The Odyssey of
THE BEAR

The Odyssey of
THE
BEAR

The Making of the Film
by Jean-Jacques Annaud

by Josée Benabent-Loiseau
translated by André Aciman

With photographs by Marianne Rosenstiehl

Newmarket Press
New York

English translation copyright © 1989 by Newmarket Press. Originally published as *Les Secrets de l'ours: Le Film de Jean-Jacques Annaud,* in French, by Editions Grasset & Fasquelle © 1988.

This book published simultaneously in the United States of America and in Canada.

Front cover photograph by Marianne Rosenstiehl.

With the exception of the following, Marianne Rosenstiehl took all the photographs appearing in this book:

Jean-Jacques Annaud (pages 23, 37, 106); Xavier Castano (pages 34, 39, 40); Agence Marceline Lenoir (page 68); Renn Productions (pages 3, 14, 15, 150, 155); Jean-Philippe Varin (pages 97, 100); and Mark Wiener (page 17).

The publisher wishes to acknowledge Columbia and Tri-Star Pictures, Renn Productions, Josée Benabent-Loiseau, and Jean-Jacques Annaud for their cooperation in the publication of this book.

Library of Congress Cataloging-in-Publication Data
Benabent-Loiseau, Josée.
[Les Secrets de l'ours. English]
The odyssey of The Bear: the making of the film by Jean-Jacques Annaud /
by Josée Benabent-Loiseau; translated by André Aciman.
p.   cm.
Translation of: Les Secrets de l'ours.
ISBN 1-55704-056-7
1. Bear (Motion picture)   I. Annaud, Jean-Jacques.   II. Title.
PN1997.B3553B4613   1989
791.43'72—dc20   89-22995
CIP

Quantity Purchases

Companies, professional groups, clubs and other organizations may qualify for special terms when ordering quantities of this title. For information contact: Special Sales Dept., Newmarket Press, 18 East 48th Street, New York, New York 10017, or call (212) 832-3575.

Manufactured in the United States of America

Text design by Sylvia Glickman/Levavi & Levavi

Acknowledgments

Jean-Jacques Annaud • Claude Berri • Pierre Grunstein • Xavier Castano • Jacques Allaire • Philippe Rousselot • Noëlle Boisson • Arnaud du Boisberranger, a dear friend, who was accidentally killed in Paris a year after the shooting of the film • Doug Seus • Lynne Seus • Clint Youngreen

and in alphabetical order:

Madame Annaud • Baldwyn • Gérard Brach • Frédéric Carol • Chris Carr • Laurence Duval • Patrick Fabre • Roberto Garzelli • Isabelle Henry • Dr. François Hugues • ICC Productions • Corinne Jorry • Tchéky Karyo • Monique Koutnetzoff • Bertrand Laforêt • Dr. Maryvonne Leclerc-Cassan • Thierry Leportier • Toni Ludi • Neue Constantin Film Produktion • André Noël • Alexandra Nouveau • Michel Parbot • Bretislav Pojar • Laurent Quaglio • Janou Shammas • John Stephenson • Jacqueline Tolianker • Noël and Sonia Vandendries-Lestienne • Jean-Philippe Varin • Mark Wiener

and for their artistic contributions:
Bart • Douce • Grizz

Contents

Infancy of
B**THE**
B**EA**R

Jean-Jacques Annaud?

The name doesn't mean anything to Claude Berri. In cinematic circles, at the time, very few have heard the name of Annaud. But they are intrigued by a demo tape containing about fifteen commercials, all of them so funny, so powerful in their spirited promotion of such brands as Orangina, Crunches, Citroën, and Kelton that it begins making the rounds. After Jacques Perrin and Costa Gavras view it, François Truffaut plays it so many times on his editing table that he tears it to shreds. He, in his turn, mentions it to his friend Claude Berri. And that is how, one morning in 1975, the latter finds out about a young director by the name of Jean-Jacques Annaud. Within twenty minutes, Berri is totally won over. He likes Annaud's visual creativity, his ideas, his "touch." He is very interested in him. In a profession in which it is often prudent to play for time, Claude Berri is a producer with an ability to make a quick decision. He acts fast because he reacts instinctively, and his infatuations assume a certain urgency. He must speak to Annaud. Instantly. When he calls him to congratulate him, he realizes that he is calling at the right time. The director is getting ready to make his first feature film and, from the look of things, is facing serious financial difficulties.

At thirty-two, Jean-Jacques Annaud has already spent eight years in advertising. He has close to five hundred commercials to his credit, and, in his field, is considered a major star. When he first started, filmed commercials had yet to be liberated from the plodding world of "ads." In a domain where the anonymity of the director is more often than not the rule, he has succeeded in establishing a personal style that is new and iconoclastic. Having become a craftsman in the art of sizzling, quick-witted repartee that, in the space of fifteen to twenty seconds, creates sudden surprise, he shows an often disconcerting, sometimes troubling daring. But he has nabbed so many international prizes that he demands and obtains an exceptional amount of freedom in his work. He has made a lot of money, traveled throughout the world, known the privilege of being sought after, appreciated, spoiled, admired. Then, one day, Jean-Jacques cracks: depression. For many months, he experiences unshakable malaise, a sensation of dizzying emptiness. This man, who has been lavished with recognition, but who is very proud, is no longer happy. Advertising stifles him. It has forced him to put too high a premium on being funny. By dint of laughing at everything, he has become incapable of believing in anything at all. He feels a compelling need to express sincere, personal emotions. His only ambition is to direct his first feature film.

The story is already written. It is the story of a handful of French colonials, in Cameroon in 1915, who enjoy the best of relations with three Germans in the neighboring military outpost until they discover that their respective countries are at war with each other. He got the idea for this film ten years earlier, while on military duty as a volunteer in Africa. He was reading a book on the history of Cameroon. One line in particular fascinated him: "The resistance of the well-known Captain von Raben on the peak of the Mora." He visited the Mora and, realizing the ridiculous nature of the situation, drew a satiric tale from this miniature conflict. At the time, however, the stars of the advertising industry were completely unknown outside their own circles; and thus, confronted with people from motion pictures, the prodigy considered himself to be a beginner. Who would really be interested in this story? Nobody. From advertising, he had mastered the art of convincing stubborn clients. He loved turning around a situation with a persuasive argument and, through sheer will and obstinacy, managed to garner no less than seven co-producers for his film. Still, it is like a gigantic jigsaw puzzle without all the pieces.

It is at this point that Claude Berri calls. Jean-Jacques does not ask for anything. No need. Claude understands that he can provide the final push and, during the course of the conversation, slips in the fact that he might distribute the film through his distribution company. Without any prior thought, Claude hits on the solution. This is exactly how he likes to do things. This is

For Claude Berri, the producer of The Bear, "What matters is not how much a film costs, but how much it makes."

also how he has achieved success in his career. He wanted to be an actor, but, because no director would hire him as an actor, he became a script writer. Then he became a director, because none of the film directors believed in his screenplays. He then became a producer, because none of the financiers considered him a serious filmmaker. Finally, he became a distributor because he had had enough of waiting for others to do what he could do better himself. This freedom, which took him years to obtain, is his real success story.

In a matter of a few days, Jean-Jacques and Claude have reached an agreement for the distribution of Annaud's first feature film. Eight months later, Claude views the first scenes of *Black and White in Color*. The film is far from final editing. It is three hours long, partly in color, partly in black and white. One out of two reels is silent. When the lights come on, Claude remains quiet. For him, it is worse than disappointing, a catastrophe. He makes a few suggestions as a matter of form, but his mind is made up. Nothing can save the film. Annaud has missed his chance. When the film is released in 1976, the critics praise it, but the public concurs with Berri's evaluation and *Black and White in Color* is a flop. Two weeks after release, the film is withdrawn from circulation. Annaud faces an impasse. His best friends urge him to return to advertising. However, this defeat leaves him with mixed feelings. Although his pride is hurt, Annaud is not entirely unhappy, for he has at least succeeded in doing what he had wanted most to do. In fact, he is more puzzled than hopeless. Why such a small audience? Why the rejection when, in theaters, viewers always applaud his commercials? He used to think that movies were simply a source of pleasure. Now he begins to suspect that they are, above all, a reflection of desire.

January 1977. Having disappeared without a trace, *Black and White in Color* comes back to life along a totally unforeseen road: Hollywood. The film is cut by ten minutes and presented by the government of the Ivory Coast, which was one of the co-producers. *Black and White in Color* is nominated for the Academy Award for Best Foreign Language Film. Annaud is taken by surprise. Berri asks to see the film again immediately. Could he have been mistaken? Yes, he was wrong, and he calls Annaud to tell him so. Later, he will confess that, ever since this experience, he has resolved never to judge an unfinished film. As the weeks pass, however, Annaud is less and less persuaded that the Oscar will be his. Everyone's absolute favorite is Jean-Charles Tacchella's *Cousin, Cousine*. Thus, on the day of the Academy Awards ceremony, when Hollywood is out in full force, Jean-Jacques Annaud, who did not think it worthwhile to even make the trip to the United States, is already fast asleep in bed at his mill in France. He is still asleep when the telephone rings:

"You won."

Obviously, he thinks it is a joke and in poor taste. He hangs up. The telephone rings again. It is the producer's secretary:

"You've won the Oscar."

Shaken, Annaud continues to doubt, but turns on his radio and stays awake. At six o'clock it is in the newspaper headlines:

"Oscar: A Disappointment for France. To everyone's surprise, a film from the Ivory Coast won. For a first film, it is a unique exploit in the history of motion picture's most prestigious award."

Lying in bed, Annaud stares at his toes for a long while. He is sorry that he did not make the trip and understands that his life is in the process of changing.

In the hours that follow, his life becomes frenetic. Journalists flood his home. So many in his profession are suddenly his friends that it seems his telephone number has been released to the entire city of Paris. In twenty-four hours, Jean-Jacques Annaud has become "brilliant." Once the first rush of curiosity subsides, however, the avalanche of propositions that were supposed to follow in its wake fail to materialize.

With advertising to fall back on, he takes his time, reflects, and conceives the framework of a new film. Six months go by. In January 1978, the screenplay for *Hothead* is ready. The story centers on a soccer player who is considered a failure and who is shunned by the residents of his city, but who becomes a hero the minute he scores the decisive goal in a major-league soccer match. The film reflects Annaud's years in advertising, when clients would reject his commercials and then, months later, praise him when he won prizes—as happened at the Venice Festival the day he won the Golden Lion: he was showered with champagne and then carried on the shoulders of a client who had rejected his spot a year before.

When Jean-Jacques meets Claude Berri to tell him the plot of his new film, the men have barely seen one another since the Oscars. Between them echoes the discomforting memory of an unsuccessful venture. Annaud has not forgotten Berri's reaction to *Black and White in Color*. Also, if the two have lost touch, it is partly because the producer got involved in the most perilous adventure of his career: Roman Polanski's *Tess*. Berri had assumed all the risks for his friend of fifteen years. Initially budgeted at $4.5 million, the film eventually doubled in cost as filming progressed. Berri sank everything he owned into it, and more. When Berri meets with Annaud, Polanski is still in the process of filming. Under these conditions, it goes without saying that *Hothead* will have to do without Berri's support.

But at the meeting the producer lends him a book and arranges for him to meet the script writer Gérard Brach. Brach had written the screenplay for *Tess* and had helped conceive the story for Berri's first film, *Le Vieil Homme et l'enfant* (*The Two of Us*). A key to Berri's success is his ability to create networks among people and to encourage others in the business to discover common ground. Neither Brach nor Annaud were particularly interested in the book, which relates the adventures of a trapper and a wolf in Alaska. And yet, when Annaud is ready to say good-bye he says to the script writer:

"The only thing I enjoyed in this story was the prehistoric fear of the characters."

Brach's eyes light up.

"A prehistoric movie: would that interest you?"

"Yes," Annaud replies. "A film without dialogue."

Two days later, Brach calls:

"*Quest for Fire*. Does it ring a bell?"

Annaud knows it. He even remembers reading it as a child in comic-strip form in *Mickey Mouse* magazine.

Both men have just discovered that they share a passion for prehistory. It's decided. Together, they will adapt Rosny *aîné*'s book. They must buy the movie rights. They read works on ethnography, anthropology, geology, and ethology, and they learn more about the origins of language. All this takes months and months, which gives Jean-Jacques Annaud the time to film and edit *Hothead*. The film, in which the highly acclaimed Patrick Dewaere stars, is more warmly received. Claude Berri sees it and enjoys it. But when he is told about *Quest for Fire*, the producer steps back. He has just finished with the Dantesque epic *Tess*, and though the film is doing well, it is far from generating the fruits of its phenomenal investment. Thus, to produce a film about the dawn of human history and re-create the world as it must have been eighty thousand years ago is too much of a long shot. Berri lacks the funds to be its producer, but he will distribute it.

Annaud and Brach still do not realize the full extent of their madness. They have a grand vision for their unusual story. From the hunt for financial backers to the most minute twists and turns of a hellish shooting, Jean-Jacques Annaud is going to live through an epic experience. Threatened with cancellation ten times and rescued from extinction ten times, *Quest for Fire* is on a permanent obstacle course. At each test, the professionals expect that Annaud will break down. Not only is he able to resist, but he improvises all sorts of solutions—from replacing a producer who abandons the film to disguising eighteen Asian elephants as prehistoric mammoths, from overcoming frightful weather conditions to sending a Scottish technical crew to Canada and then to Kenya. Jean-Jacques Annaud manages this extraordinary adventure like a high-stakes poker game. He knows that if he fails he might as well return to advertising for another ten years. But he passionately believes in the film and thrives under adversity. The more complicated things are, the more stubborn he becomes. He has only one principle: "Everything is possible." When Brach writes "a mammoth" in the screenplay, Annaud sees a whole herd of them. Then he puts the apprehensive script writer at ease:

"We'll find a way, you'll see."

On November 5, 1981, a month and a half before the film is due to be released in France, Annaud shows it—this time completed—to Claude Berri, his first viewer. Berri leaves the projection room raving. He makes ten consecutive calls to announce the good news. That evening, from his home, he calls Annaud. Not given, as a rule, to rhetorical flourishes, he exclaims:

"Your name will be written in gold in the history of motion pictures. You've just made a classic. Let's meet tomorrow."

The next day, Claude Berri comes straight to the point:

"I'll produce your next film. You've got carte blanche."

No one, at the time he announces his decision, knows for sure that *Quest for Fire* will be an international success. But Claude Berri is not the sort of man to question his own infatuations. He loved what he saw on the screen and admires Annaud's achievement so far. That's enough. Doubtless, his wholesale confidence in Annaud is also his way of letting bygones be bygones. What remains now is to liquidate the liabilities of *Black and White in Color*. This gesture moves the director and takes him by surprise. What film would he like to direct now? He doesn't know.

After the challenge of *Quest for Fire*, he feels ready to undertake others and, without waiting, mentions this to Gérard Brach.

Beyond the friendship, which binds them from now on, both men share a taste for topics that are regarded as "impossible." Brach, who fears crowded streets and lives cloistered in his home, escapes through his imagination. Annaud, far from channeling the rovings of his imagination, spurs them on. It is in this manner that they were able to create *Quest for Fire*. It is in the same spirit that they wish to repeat the experiment.

The film director would like to work on a popular, family-oriented theme. Brach asks for a few days to think about it. While rummaging through his books, he comes upon a forgotten novel, *The Grizzly King*, by James Oliver Curwood, and skims it mechanically. He begins to recall forgotten images. He starts it from the beginning and reads it in one sitting: fascinating.

He sends it to Jean-Jacques Annaud with the following message: "Read this book. I loved it as a boy."

The director is enthusiastic about the book. The story is very simple. The animals are the protagonists. For Annaud, this is where the challenge resides. He must create a story in which the spectator will identify with the bears, share their joys, their suffering, their fears, and their struggles, and wish for their victory. Brach and Annaud understand each other perfectly. They begin to dream of a film whose title would be, very simply, *The Bear*. While the script writer immediately sits down to write it, the director packs his bags for a trip that begins in November 1981 and ends in March 1982, and that takes him around the world, wherever *Quest for Fire* is released. For Annaud, promotion is the exact opposite of drudgery. It is not an obligation; rather, it represents the last act of the film's adventure. The more crowded his schedule is, the happier he is. From morning till night, he relates the story of his epic, astutely learning to respond to interviewers' capricious questions. In short, he becomes a European media phenomenon.

Between two airplanes, just in time for a brief stop in Paris, Annaud runs to Gérard Brach's home, reads the latest pages of the screenplay, makes some suggestions, and rushes out.

In April 1982, he gives himself a pause: two weeks in Guadeloupe, where he nevertheless manages to grant four or five interviews. One morning he reads in *Le Monde* a small note announcing the forthcoming publication of Umberto Eco's latest book. Its title is strange: *The Name of the Rose*. The description of its theme is unusual: "a Gothic detective novel about laughter." A puzzling

Gérard Brach and Annaud begin to dream about a film that would be simply entitled The Bear.

association of words. Soon, the director places a call to his oldest friend, the script writer Alain Godard, and asks him to buy the novel. Why? Out of sheer curiosity. Two days later, Godard calls back. The novel, which he devoured in two nights, is unlike any other he has read. Nothing else is necessary to send Annaud into a state of alert. He cuts short his trip, returns to Paris, and plunges into the book. This subject, at once ambitious and accessible, learned and popular, unleashes an unusual excitement in him. He has but one thought: to obtain the movie rights. Jean-Jacques gets in touch with his agent, who makes the necessary inquiries. Bad news: Italian television has already signed the contract. Annaud replies:

"Then I must meet Eco. Find a way."

Obviously, Gérard Brach is the first person who hears of Annaud's new passion. He talks about *The Name of the Rose* with such ardor that the script writer is led to believe that Annaud might want to drop *The Bear*. Wrong: work on *The Bear* must continue, but Annaud has decided to do whatever it takes to direct *The Name of the Rose*.

In May 1982, Jean-Jacques Annaud is on the jury of the thirty-fifth Cannes Film Festival. He speaks with Gérard Lebovici, one of French cinema's mythic figures. As the founder of the French agency Artmédia, which he started at the suggestion of his longtime friend Claude Berri, he has managed to gather the cream of France's actors and directors. His enemies speak about him with grave consternation, his friends would follow him blindfolded, and strangers wonder how to establish contact with him. "Lebo" is powerful, an intransigent and passionate figure. Moreover, he's a fearsome businessman. Just before the festival, he leaves Artmédia to create his own production and distribution firm, AAA. He wants to start his new company with a bang. He has not read *The Name of the Rose* but he is extremely interested in the man who filmed *Quest for Fire*. In the face of Annaud's enthusiasm, "Lebo" senses a big hit. As soon as he returns to Paris, he devours Umberto Eco's book, contacts the Italian television company to buy back the rights, and informs Jean-Jacques Annaud that he wants to produce his movie.

Only one shadow lingers: What becomes of Claude Berri in this whole affair? Annaud lets him know of Lebovici's offer. Berri is hardly worried, since the rights are blocked. Besides, *The Bear* is progressing. No need to panic.

In June 1982, Annaud leaves for Australia, where *Quest for Fire* is about to be released. He takes Gérard Brach's thirty-five-page synopsis of *The Bear* with him. As he reads it on the airplane, Annaud begins to pale: the script writer has introduced material that seems to undermine the theme of the story as they originally discussed it. Once in Sydney, he spends the entire night writing, twenty-four tightly written pages in which he refutes, argues with, and dissects the synopsis. As is his habit, he writes whatever ideas come to mind, things he feels, thoughts he has. Most of the time, he never rereads his notes. It is enough for him to know they exist. This time, however, and after many days of hesitation, he decides to mail them to Brach. Once in Paris, he waits eight days for an answer that never comes, before picking up the telephone himself. They plan a meeting. The discussion is lengthy and chaotic.

Each defends his own point of view, criticizes the other's, and justifies again, point by point, his own. This great outpouring is not futile. Gradually, Brach begins to define the story that Annaud wants to tell. It can be told in very few words, the same ones that Annaud uses in Claude Berri's office the next day:

"Here is the subject: an orphan bear cub; a large solitary bear; two hunters; the animals' point of view."

Berri nods his head, a glimmer of jubilation in his eyes: "It's one of the most beautiful stories I've ever heard."

Toward the end of the summer, the screenplay for *The Bear* begins to take shape. From Curwood's novel, Annaud and Brach have retained little more than certain descriptions of the Canadian north, where the action takes place. Using the framework of the novel, they weave their own interpretations, invent scenes, create new situations, with only one guiding principle, the same one as always: "Everything is possible."

It is also toward the end of the summer that Jean-Jacques Annaud gets some good news: he has an appointment scheduled with Umberto Eco in mid-September. During his dinner at the writer's home in Milan, the director decides to risk everything. He has read and reread *The Name of the Rose* so many times that he is able to discuss it scene by scene and to describe, one after the another, its many characters. He asserts that the novel was conceived and written for him, that ever since childhood he has nursed a passion for the Middle Ages—which is true—and that this era has often been misrepresented in motion pictures. He tells how at the age of eight, with his Brownie camera, he was already taking pictures of all the churches in France, and that, while on vacation, he would have his parents drive miles out of their way to see a relic. That, at the age of eleven, with his super-eight movie camera, he produced his first film, naively and pompously titled "A Documentary on Romanesque Frescoes in Saint-Savin-sur-Gartempe."

The money? He will find it. He is already thinking about it. The historical accuracy? Background material has been piling up on his desk for several months. He swears that he will find the leather out of which Franciscans used to make their sandals, and the exact size of a Benedictine's tonsure. He will even go as far as Assisi to see the cowl of Saint Francis. Italian television would turn this novel into a six-hour serialized wasteland; he would turn it into a two-hour cinematographic marvel. Umberto Eco enjoys himself and is moved.

And so on October 1982 Gérard Lebovici and Jean-Jacques Annaud obtain the rights to adapt *The Name of the Rose*.

Now they have to break the news to Claude Berri. Lebovici can wait no longer. He invites him to dinner and tells him:

"You have the rights to *The Bear*, and I have *The Name of the Rose*. It is up to Jean-Jacques to decide which one he wants to begin with."

Berri seethes with rage. As soon as he returns to his office, he writes an inflammatory letter to Lebovici. He feels betrayed by his friend of thirty years, whom he's known since their school days and with whom he shares an almost brotherly friendship. Three days later, however, he sends a second letter renouncing the first. Friendship is more powerful than rancor. That's how Berri is: impetuous, impassioned, easily angered, but generous to a fault.

The one who holds the key to the problem is Jean-Jacques Annaud. Without hesitating, he undertakes both projects at once. Juggling is part of a tightrope walker's act. Annaud has a good sense of balance, a cast-iron will, nerves of steel, a mind that works with a computerlike precision, and an uncanny ability to let his commitments proliferate. Everyone predicts that he won't make it. Jean-Jacques Annaud responds with military-style organization. His schedule is diabolical. In the same day, he can work with Brach in the morning; have lunch with Claude Berri; spend the afternoon with Alain Godard, totally immersed in the adaptation of *The Name of the Rose;* and have dinner with Lebovici. When he is not writing, he rummages through mountains of background material. He takes notes, clips articles, photocopies, files, all with the precision of a diligent student. This is his weakness, the "teacher's pet" side of him—and he enjoys flaunting it, too.

Born in Draveil, twenty minutes outside of Paris, on October 1, 1943, Annaud defines himself as "a pure suburbanite." His father worked for the railroad and his mother was a corporate secretary; they both took him to the movies once a week, on Sundays.

He was seven years old when he received in the mail his first weekly *Mickey Mouse* magazine, in which he passionately followed the prehistoric comic-strip adventures based on the book *Quest for Fire*. In the same mail he discovered the camera catalog his mother subscribed to, and it fascinated him. He knew those objects were responsible for the films that brought him so much pleasure on Sunday afternoons. He instantly knew that he wanted to play with these machines and create the same feeling in others. He started collecting old movie projectors and amateur movie cameras; his urge to create movies had found its birth.

After graduating first in his class from the Vaugirard School, which specializes in the technical aspects of filmmaking, he entered I.D.H.E.C. (the Higher Institute of Cinematographic Studies) and graduated at the age of twenty. At the same time, he graduated with a B.A. in literature from the Sorbonne, studying Greek, aesthetics, theatrical studies, medieval history, and the history of medieval art.

And despite the commercial success of *Quest for Fire*, on this December day in 1982, Jean-Jacques Annaud is feeling relatively uncertain. The challenge represented by the adaptation of *The Name of the Rose* is like the novel itself: monumental, abundant, proliferating. Eco mixes a multitude of themes, and tangles the threads of a complex plot at whim. Annaud must prune the story without betraying the text. How?

While Annaud and Godard throw into the trash the first draft of *The Name of the Rose*, Brach and Annaud deliver the completed screenplay of *The Bear* to Claude Berri. For the producer, the 120-page screenplay measures up to what he had imagined. As he reads it, he delights in the adventures of the hero, Youk, the bear cub who watches his mother die, crushed by a falling rock, and who is taken under the care of Kaar, a colossal, solitary bear. The latter is wounded, and two hunters, Tom and Bill, are tracking him. The bears must flee. From the hunters' viewpoint, the relentless will to kill is depicted; from the bear's, cunning, familiarity with the terrain, a faultless sense of smell; and from the cub's, the discovery of life: from the joy of play, the defense of territory, the lesson in survival before a raging puma, the fear when pursued by a pack of dogs who are hungry for blood, to the discovery of lovemaking when he watches Kaar seduce Iskwao, an irresistibly sexy she-bear. A subtle relationship grows between the cub and the old bear, and then, little by little, between the hunters and the hunted: human intelligence confronted with animal instinct.

Berri knows that he is reading an exceptional story in which the images, the sounds, and the music will relate the actions of the animals, their feelings, and their emotions.

How does one put animals onscreen? This completely puzzles Berri. How will Annaud go about transforming a bear cub into a star? The producer is willing to pay dearly to see this happen. This is what he tells Pierre Grunstein when he gives the go-ahead to start the preparations for the film. For twenty years, Grunstein has been one of the pillars of Renn Productions, Claude Berri's company. After having been Berri's assistant on his first film, *The Two of Us*, Grunstein became his trusted friend and associate producer. He is the one who prepares the cost estimates and who tracks the progress of the films from the very first detail to the very last. Berri does not involve himself in such things. What he likes to do is produce stories that excite him and to set up the financing for them. What matters most is not so much finding the money as spending it. He has only one concern: giving the film the greatest possible chance of succeeding, which to his mind means granting the film director all the means and support he needs. "The opposite of wasting," he likes to repeat. Let Pierre Grunstein translate his desires into numbers.

The associate producer knows the importance that Claude Berri attaches to this film by the sheer fact that he has been hearing about it for eighteen months. And he too, upon finishing the screenplay, experiences Berri's pleasure. In contradistinction to the modern world's excess of violent images and surfeit of information, this story represents a return to silence, to nature, to the art of looking. For thirty years he has been rubbing shoulders with actors, tempering their whims and their demands, but *The Bear* opens a new vista.

Where, and how, will they find these plantigrade animals? To what inaccessible corners of the world will the director have to go in order to locate the uninhabited territory required by the screenplay? How many months will have to be spent exploring, developing procedures, doing research, before they will be ready to start filming? For Grunstein, this film is a voyage into unknown territory, requiring budgeting without guidelines—impossible to determine beforehand: in short, an unusual, hence exciting, undertaking.

When on February 23, 1983, he flies to New Zealand with Jean-Jacques Annaud, he is certain of only one thing: his troubles have just begun.

Why go to this country at the other end of the world? Because the director remembers the lake and mountain regions, whose terrain is wild and unspoiled. Once there, they find that the area has been invaded by sheep. Those rare spots that are without flocks are inaccessible. From there they go to Australia, flying over marvelous nature preserves. But these areas are lacking in hotel accommodations.

They head for California. Now it is a question of selecting bears. The search begins poorly. The bears that Jean-Jacques Annaud and Pierre Grun-

February, 1983. Casting for bears in California, Pierre Grunstein, the associate producer, on the left, is sure of only one thing: his troubles have just begun.

stein meet are pitiful. They are so domesticated, having served so many advertisers, filmmakers, and television producers, that they have lost their claws, their teeth, and their personalities. Annaud and Grunstein are on the verge of heading back to France, without having found any bears or a film location, when the Society for Animal Actors gives them the names of two bear trainers with excellent reputations.

The first, Doug Seus, lives in Utah, thirty miles from Salt Lake City, in a suburb called Heber. Next to his house is a sign announcing his corporate identity: WASATCH ROCKY MOUNTAIN WILDLIFE, INC. The man who opens the door is a giant with a golden beard who looks as though he has just escaped from a Western set in the days of the Gold Rush. Next to him is Lynne, his wife, a charming woman with witty round blue eyes, and his son-in-law, Clint Youngreen, large and amiable-looking.

The arrival of the foreigners has created some excitement among the members of the family. The sign indicates wildlife. In fact, they hear roaring in the small garden behind the house.

"It's Bart," says Doug Seus simply.

Upon seeing the animal, Annaud and Grunstein step back. The trainer reassures them: Bart is very sociable. But he is impressive all the same: a monumental bear, a Kodiak. Doug tells them Bart's size, and Annaud translates for Grunstein: nine feet, two thousand pounds. Bart is six years old. For the past three years, he has starred in numerous commercials and films.

Taken aback by the size of the animal, Annaud asks to see him work. Right off, Bart demonstrates his friendship for his master. Standing on his rear paws, he hugs Doug Seus with his front paws and gently puts him down again. He rolls him on the ground, has fun putting Doug's arm into his mouth, hugs him tightly, sniffs at his hair.

"Stop, Bart, let's go to work."

Immediately, the bear steps back and follows orders.

"Stay. Up. Sit. Smile. Back. Go to bed."

It's not that Bart goes back into his cage to sleep. No. He lies down on his back, spreads his limbs, and stays absolutely still. His perfect docility impresses the film director, who thinks that Bart would make an ideal Kaar. Jean-Jacques and Pierre Grunstein purchase an option. For the next two hours, the film director, with the screenplay in his hand, will explain Kaar's role to Doug Seus. While he is satisfied with Bart's capacity for showing tenderness, he asks the trainer to teach him the gestures of violence and aggression necessary for the development of the story.

The next day they return to California. An hour's car ride from Los Angeles, near the town of Acton, in the Central Valley, a road sign says: STEVE MARTIN'S WORKING WILDLIFE. In the middle of a huge area surrounded by snow-capped mountains, Steve Martin lives in a prefabricated house. Nearby, a trailer doubles as his office. Behind it are dozens of cages, containing 150 animals of all species: parrots, monkeys, tigers, panthers . . . In a small pool two seals circle each other. It is a preserve for animal "actors," and Hollywood filmmakers regularly employ them. Martin, it turns out, is a businessman who welcomes the director's visit as a good business opportunity.

A bearded, forty-year-old man named Mark Wiener is in charge of training the animals. He is warm and immediately starts asking questions about the film. He takes the visitors to a cage where a bear sways distrustfully, and he warns them to stay away as he releases the bear. This Kodiak, called Doc

16

(he is, in fact, Bart's brother), does not look comfortable. Even Mark Wiener approaches him cautiously. Doc is tense, apprehensive. At nine feet and fifteen hundred pounds, he has a savage liveliness that, for the director, contrasts sharply with his brother's docility. When asked to perform, he reveals impressive talents. He responds to a vocabulary of forty words, smiles, stands

March, 1983. In California, the trainer Mark Weiner shows off Bart's brother, Doc, who will be Bart's stand-in.

Grizz, an effeminate male grizzly, will play the alluring Iskwao, whom Kaar will seduce.

up, sits down, pushes a pole, runs, climbs, wrinkles his nose, sniffs. Jean-Jacques deems that Doc would make a wonderful understudy for Bart.

In the next cage, languidly slumped on the floor, is a sprawling grizzly. With his pointed muzzle, lightly rounded ears, and eyes that look as though they're made up with black eyeshadow, Grizz is a very effeminate male, a sexy, attractive, expressive, and devilish vamp. Jean-Jacques Annaud thinks he would be perfect for the role of the enticing Iskwao, Kaar's "girlfriend." In two days' time, the casting has been worked out quite well, and Pierre Grunstein is surprised to see things progressing with such apparent ease.

After stopping in Las Vegas to view some circus bears who turn out to be of no interest, they go to Montana to see David Peacock, a Vietnam veteran who for the past ten years has specialized in the behavior of bears. He is an outdoorsman who spends weeks on end with a 16-mm camera filming the grizzlies in Yellowstone National Park. He has produced a large number of impressive documentaries, and his advice will prove to be extremely useful. Peacock confirms what the director already knows from his own reading. First, it might be dangerous for a bear cub to work closely with an adult bear that is not its mother. This doesn't deter Annaud. The greater the challenge, the happier he is. But for security, he thinks he should mix fake bears with the real ones in some of the intimate scenes and close-ups.

The film director is thinking of mechanical devices, or of mimes who could be trained to act the part of bears while wearing artificial bearskins—or of both at the same time. Pierre Grunstein tries to imagine what sort of work that would entail. He knows that the apparent simplicity of the screenplay conceals pitfalls.

On April 6, at Pinewood Studios, in the suburbs of London, Jean-Jacques Annaud and Pierre Grunstein meet with Rick Baker during the shooting of *Tarzan: The Legend of Greystoke*. It was he who built the fake gorillas for that film. They are superb. Baker, who won an Oscar for *An American Werewolf in London*, is such a perfectionist that he demanded that each hair of the gorillas' fur be individually glued to the skin. He is not afraid of bears, but he is so exhausted by the intensive work for *Greystoke* that he declines Annaud's offer. Annaud, however, has not made this trip for nothing. On the set, he finds Ailsa Berk. She is a mime who played the role of one of the women in Ulam's tribe in *Quest for Fire*. During training the director had immediately noticed her wonderful sense for the right movement. She is not afraid of bears and, moreover, is very enthusiastic about the project. She is ready to take a screen test without further ado.

Within twenty-four hours, Pierre Grunstein is able to "borrow" from a London zoo a tame bear, who is brought right to the doorstep of the studio. In a corner of the *Greystoke* set, Ailsa Berk observes the animal for a few minutes and then begins her imitation. Bent over, resting both arms on two steel extensions, she mimics the bear's gait, his manner of swaying while moving: a mimetic exercise of fascinating precision. The spectators are enthralled, and Jean-Jacques Annaud hires her on the spot. Ailsa Berk will coordinate the work performed by the mimes who will be chosen to play the fake bears.

The Bear or *The Name of the Rose?* *The Name of the Rose* or *The Bear?* Annaud does not ask questions. Not yet. He continues to oscillate between one project and the other with equal energy. Back in France, he begins working on the storyboards for *The Bear;* that is, on drawings that illustrate—scene by scene—the screenplay. This method allows him to spell out his ideas on paper while defining the frame and the position of the cameras. Then Annaud goes to discuss the new version of *The Name of the Rose* with Alain Godard, and the third, fourth, fifth versions. By the sixth, summer is drawing to a close and Godard founders. The basic structure of the screenplay is established, but the director thinks that a fresh pair of eyes are needed to give it a new emotional impact. Why not the eyes of Gérard Brach? Since he has just finished writing *The Bear,* he could devote himself to *The Name of the Rose.* In this way, everything will remain in the family. Brach, stimulated by the new challenge, tackles the seventh version.

In mid-September 1983, Jean-Jacques Annaud leaves for Vancouver with Pierre Grunstein. In British Columbia both men visit wonderful landscapes. The farther north they head, the more they feel they are stepping into the scenery for the film. They go as far as the town of Inuvik, on the edge of the Arctic Ocean near the Alaskan border.

One morning, Annaud, Grunstein, and a Canadian set designer leave by helicopter to fly over the Beaufort Sea and its stretches of glaciers. The weather is superb, and the landscape lunar. By mid-morning, the director asks the pilot to land on top of one of the glaciers to take pictures. The door opens, the wind sweeps through the cabin, and the navigation map flies away. They run across the ice, in vain. The pilot does not panic. He knows the area well and decides to fly slightly farther, to Wainwright, the last American base, facing the Soviet Union on the other side of the Bering Strait. An officer agrees to give up a map. It's old, but it's better than nothing. The hours pass. The chopper stops often. Annaud takes dozens of pictures. Around 3:00 P.M. they head back to Inuvik.

Pierre Grunstein falls asleep. When he wakes up, night has fallen. There are glaciers everywhere. The passengers exchange apprehensive glances. Deathly pale, the pilot confesses that he is lost. Send for help? Impossible. The radio is not working. The gas tank is almost empty. No one speaks. There is silent panic, intense cold. For the tenth time, the set designer who accompanies them rereads the map. He locates a minuscule spot on it that indicates a beacon and, with his compass, guides the pilot. When the chopper finally lands in Inuvik, the gas-tank gauge is hovering below empty.

The pilot, who until then has been silent, explains that he confused the Mackenzie Mountains and the Beaufort Sea. He also hands them his bill. This is his last mistake. Pierre Grunstein, who speaks rudimentary English, nevertheless finds words with which to insult him.

Except for this misadventure, the assessment of the trip is positive. Immense wild spaces, forests that go on forever, dotted by lakes, mountains whose peaks rise above thirteen thousand feet, not to mention the surreal autumnal light of Canada: all these fit perfectly well with the picture Annaud has for his film. But he must also keep in mind another dimension: the rate of the dollar. At this time, it is very high. According to his initial estimates, the budget for filming in British Columbia will be approximately $25 million! And there are still many unknowns.

The amount is so astronomical that, from now on, only Claude Berri can decide whether to continue with the preparations. Since becoming a film producer, Berri has always held fast to one principle: never hamstring a director financially. According to Berri, what matters is not how much a film costs, but how much it may earn. This time, however, he deems the investment staggering, above his means. If shooting could be done in Europe, the cost would be significantly less. They still must locate adequate sites. Where should they look? Pierre Grunstein sends a set designer to scout the Spanish side of the Pyrenees and the Hungarian portion of the Carpathians. The landscapes are too tame for a story requiring such imposing vistas. The project stalls. For the first time, Claude Berri wonders whether he will be able to carry it off. Annaud as well thinks the budget for *The Bear* may be too high.

This may be a turning point in his race between his two projects, especially since, contemporaneously, Brach has achieved wonders with the screenplay for *The Name of the Rose*. Now he must make a decision.

Annaud has already made his choice when he invites Claude Berri to dinner on January 24, 1984. For a variety of reasons, he will give priority to *The Name of the Rose*. If he directs *The Bear* after *Quest for Fire*, he will risk being typecast as an "animal filmmaker." Also, he wants to work with a text and with actors, and to escape, for the time being, from nature and its vast, empty expanses. It's a matter of personal balance.

Claude Berri understands, but he is not the sort of man to give up without one last try. He asks Pierre Grunstein to scout locations again in British Columbia and Annaud to look up the trainers in the United States to establish as precise a cost estimate as possible. In light of the estimate, he will decide whether or not to pursue the project. Annaud agrees to postpone his own decision until then.

On February 23, 1984, Pierre Grunstein leaves for British Columbia. But snow conditions are such that it is impossible to explore anything at all. The roads are impassable. In these regions, snow falls until the summer, and the only way of reaching a possible film location would be by helicopter. One doesn't need to be a genius with numbers to imagine the cost of having to transport by chopper, every day, the bears, the technical crew, and the equipment. Pierre Grunstein shudders at the mere thought.

When he meets Annaud at Doug Seus's home, in Utah, Jean-Jacques is not beaming with optimism. But he pretends. For five days he will explain to the trainer every sketch in the storyboards, defining, scene by scene, what he expects of the bear. Bart will have to learn to limp, to roll in water, to hold a fish in his mouth without eating it, to have a fake wound in his shoulder, to climb and come down steep slopes. For Doug Seus, nothing is impossible. All that's needed is time. As for filming real and fake bears together, the trainer is categorical: it is out of the question for fake bears to be built with real fur. Bears have poor vision but a highly developed sense of smell. If Bart smelled a real skin, he would immediately throw himself on it. How about synthetic fur? Annaud makes a face. At this point Grunstein interjects his "small" budget problem from among a list of all those that trouble him.

On May 6, 1984, Pierre Grunstein and Jean-Jacques Annaud leave Utah for Los Angeles. At 3:00 A.M. the telephone rings in the director's room at the Westwood Marquis. It is a call from France. Very bad news. Gérard Lebovici, the producer of *The Name of the Rose*, has just been killed by four shots from a twenty-two-caliber rifle in his parking lot on the avenue Foch in Paris. This was the man with whom Annaud had started the adventure enthusiastically and then had pursued it, through various difficulties, despite the brusque quality for which "Lebo" was famous.

At that moment, it is difficult to imagine all the consequences of the murder.

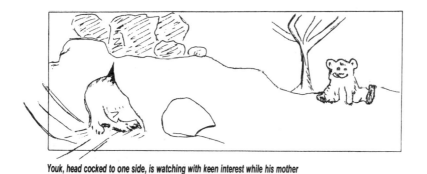

In the summer of 1983, Annaud begins to sketch out detailed scenes for The Bear,
and ultimately he creates 1700
storyboards.

2. WS reverse shot.

*Youk, head cocked to one side, is watching with keen interest while his mother
engages in an important quest.*

3. LS. Youk stares intently.

*Youk the bear cub has round ears and a pot belly, and his eyes are as bright as
slivers of obsidian.*

4. LS mother bear wriggles out of
the hole, back to camera.

NB. Set up dressing room for
trainer inside rocks

*The greedy she-bear, with her thick black coat of fur, has burrowed beneath the
mass of loose stone and is now extricating herself backwards, licking skeins of
yellow honey from her chops.*

5. LS bees swarming out of the
cave when the she-bear has
wriggled out of the rocks.

A fatalist, Annaud tells himself that by staying a few more days in California, he could try to interest other studios in his project and thus give Pierre Grunstein the time to establish the definitive budget for *The Bear*. Annaud gets in touch with Fox, and Grunstein juggles the dollar figures. The executives of Fox do not close the door on a more detailed discussion of *The Name of the Rose*. Pierre Grunstein sees no way to do *The Bear*. He calls Claude Berri to tell him that in his opinion the project cannot be undertaken under the present conditions. He quotes figures and lists the problems that have yet to be resolved. Berri agrees. Besides, how could he commit himself to such a project when he has just started another enormous one with a colossal budget: the production of *Jean de Florette* and *Manon of the Spring*? Pierre Grunstein knows better than anyone else that Berri, who is carried away by Pagnol's novel, will from now on be preoccupied with this new passion.

At the end of this lengthy conversation, a decision is made: Claude Berri authorizes Pierre Grunstein to release Jean-Jacques Annaud. No, he is not giving up. He is merely postponing his project.

The associate producer then gets in touch with Doug Seus and asks him to undertake the training of the bear according to the director's specifications, even though the actual filming has been postponed until an unknown date. Then he tells Mark Wiener, the other trainer, that he will get in touch with him later.

Eight days later, Jean-Jacques Annaud is having lunch with Pierre Hebey. Hebey, a respected lawyer who represented Lebovici's interests, has now taken Lebovici's place at the helm of AAA. From its inception, he had supported the film project. He promises to see it through and will keep his word. Jean-Jacques Annaud prepares for *The Name of the Rose*.

During the two years that follow, he will not have a day's rest. From the choice of Sean Connery as the film's star to the search for an abbey, from the construction of the scenery to the casting of the monks and the assembling of the crew, Jean-Jacques Annaud travels the world with the goal of reconciling two requirements: entertainment and originality. He himself will try to find the $19 million required for the undertaking. It is finally a German producer, Bernd Eichinger, who assumes the greatest part of the financial risk, helped by the participation of American, British, Italian, and French investors. Shooting, which starts near Frankfurt on November 11, 1985, ends in Italy on March 20, 1986.

In February, Annaud calls his agent in Paris from Rome and talks with him again about *The Bear*. Claude Berri, who is immersed in the shooting of Pagnol's saga, patiently awaits the completion of the finishing touches of *The Name of the Rose*, due to be released in mid-August. On August 28, the day after the triumphant release of *Jean de Florette*, he calls Pierre Grunstein: "We now have a project that I value very much. It's *The Bear*. Start preparations for it."

The past few months have exhausted Pierre. The stifling heat of the hills of Provence, the endless search for hundreds of extras, the demands of Claude Berri, the olive tree plantations, the hundreds of rows of tomatoes, the fifteen thousand carnations, the watering of fields, the building of roads to reach the film set—in short, the thousand and one problems raised by *Jean de Florette* have tired him out. He has only one dream: to take a vacation. But the prospect of starting the preparations for *The Bear* gives him a burst of energy. He reaches Jean-Jacques Annaud, who is in the United States promoting *The Name of the Rose*, and raises once again the question of the film's location, just as though they were picking up a conversation that had been barely interrupted.

"And why not Utah," says Pierre, "where our star lives? That would make things quite a bit simpler."

Because the dollar has fallen significantly over the past three years, it becomes less unreasonable to consider filming in the United States. As soon as he has finished with his press conferences, Annaud goes to Utah. The landscape, though spectacular, is unfit for the requirements of the script. He tours Alaska, visits the national parks of Banff and Jasper: breathtaking landscapes, but inaccessible except by helicopter. Then he leaves for Oregon, where the vistas are empty and flat. Pierre Grunstein begins to worry again and thinks that if the film does not get going now, it never will. The preparations linger, especially since Jean-Jacques Annaud becomes extremely busy. *The Name of the Rose* has just been released in Europe, and its director is going from country to country, devoting himself to it exclusively. He is in Austria on October 17, in Italy on the nineteenth, in Germany on the twenty-first. And then a miracle occurs. As he is crossing the Bavarian Alps, Jean-Jacques is dazzled by the majestic forests, speckled with lakes, and the mysterious valleys. He has found the setting for *The Bear*.

Back in Paris, he shares his impressions with Pierre Grunstein, who is relieved to hear what he has to say and finds the idea excellent. On October

30, Annaud leaves to scout for locations. In ten days, he finds magnificent sites around Garmisch-Partenkirchen, in the Isar Valley in Germany, and immense uninhabited expanses in Austria around Innsbruck, Salzburg, and Lienz. He returns to Paris with a set of dazzling pictures. Two days later, Pierre Grunstein packs and leaves, hot on the trail. Impressed by the wild beauty of the landscape, he calls Claude Berri and announces that his *Bear* is doing well.

The machine starts churning. Xavier Castano, a friend and regular visitor in the Berri home, is hired as first assistant director. After having participated in the mad capers of *Jean de Florette* and *Manon of the Spring*, he is frightened of nothing.

In turn, he goes to Germany and Austria to scout locations. But within ten days snow appears, and certain areas become inaccessible. Pierre Grunstein summons the American trainers Doug Seus and Mark Wiener. Doug has been training his bear for three years now. Bart has made considerable progress and continues to improve his mastery of the part as outlined in the storyboards. The trainer is delighted to hear that the project has been reactivated, but categorically opposes having to film in Europe. His bear has traveled only between Salt Lake City and Los Angeles and is not up to crossing the Atlantic. Pierre Grunstein panics. How can they do without such a star? He gets in touch with Mark Wiener and makes certain that both his bears—Doc and Grizz—are available. The bears are not otherwise engaged and would be delighted to work in Germany and Austria. The world of trainers is very small, and the rivalries are deep. As soon as he hears the news, Doug Seus calls Pierre Grunstein, agrees to the conditions, and contacts his lawyer to draw up a contract.

Pierre Grunstein hires Jacques Allaire as the animal manager. He must find Youk's mother, a pack of dogs, a number of other animals, but especially Youk, the bear cub. Annaud would like to have about fifteen cubs available, if possible, each with a different personality, in order to use the skills of each to create one Youk. In any event, it is imperative to establish a rotation system so as not to expose the cubs to excessive fatigue. Jacques Allaire is going to scout in France, Poland, Hungary, Italy, and Czechoslovakia—a particularly difficult task, especially since Christmas is approaching and during this period all the circuses are on tour. As for the cubs, the animal manager gets in touch with the zoos in Thoiry, Saint-Vrain, Peaugres, Vichy, Nancy, as well as in Hannover, London, Madrid, Munich, and Genk. All of them are expecting births in January 1987.

At the same time, Jean-Philippe Varin is hired as a zoological advisor. A biologist by training, Varin produced two hundred films in Africa before settling in Sologne in 1980. He built a house of 8,500 square feet surrounded by fifteen acres of land and ponds and inhabited by hundreds of animals. He is asked to care for the bear cubs until filming begins.

Varin introduces Grunstein and Allaire to Drs. François Hugues and Maryvonne Leclerc-Cassan, both of whom are affiliated with the Vincennes zoo, which is expecting cub births between the end of December and mid-January. On this afternoon, the film people will be taught the essentials of what they need to know: the she-bears are fertile in the spring. Coupling occurs not in one day but over a period of days. Pregnancy lasts anywhere from six to nine months. At birth, the cubs are as small as rats, are blind, and weigh between seven and fourteen ounces.

The two veterinarians have been conducting research on bears for years. Enthralled by the subject of the film, they offer to care for the bear cubs due to be born in the Vincennes zoo. Ordinarily, either the newborns will be cared for by the mother, who will leave the nest when the cubs are two months old, or they will be abandoned by the mother as soon as they are born. In the latter case, the doctors will use a method they call "impregnation," which consists of recovering the newborn cubs and raising them artificially. This creates serious problems, for at that stage the cubs are unfinished embryos and are susceptible to pulmonary ailments. In addition, since cubs are often mistreated by the mother, they may sustain internal injuries and irreversible lesions that become clinically evident in a few days and bring about sudden death.

As soon as the females seem to have lost interest in their offspring, the two doctors are ready to attempt this method, thus assuring the cubs shelter, proper feeding, and medical attention. Pierre Grunstein approves the offer of the veterinarians, whose reputations are unquestioned among specialists.

The preparation progresses. There remains one problem: how to construct the fake bears.

Ailsa Berk, who had been hired in 1983 and, since then, had played the role of the fake monkey in Oshima's film *Max mon amour*, feels ready to start training the mimes.

But who will manufacture the fake bears? After exploring various possibilities, Annaud thinks of contacting Jim Henson. Henson is the creator of "The Muppet Show," and is also the inventor of "animatronics," a technique that permits the remote-control animation of objects and figures. This is how he produced *The Dark Crystal*, the first film in which the characters were played entirely by mechanized figures.

On December 7, Jean-Jacques Annaud leaves for London with Xavier Castano and Pierre Grunstein. In Hampstead, north of London, on the doorway to a red brick home, a sign reads: PRIVATE HENSON ORGANIZATION. NO SMOKING. As soon as introductions are made, Annaud describes his project to the English crew. He explains why animatronics is indispensable to the success of his project. Since he has a very precise idea of the scenes he wants to film with real bears, he would like to use the fake ones as doubles, in case difficulties crop up, especially in wide-angle shots and close-ups.

After highlighting these general points, the film director describes the characters to be manufactured: Kaar; Iskwao, his girlfriend; Youk and his mother. Then he explains some of the more complicated sequences on the storyboards. This first discussion lasts three hours, during which Jean-Jacques does not stop speaking. He explains in detail his intentions, which he has been polishing and repolishing for close to four years. Impressed, the English team looks at this self-assured man, thinks he is even crazier than other film directors, and shares his enthusiasm for the project.

From London, Annaud flies back to Paris. *The Name of the Rose* is to be released in France in ten days, and the director is caught up in the promotion. In between two appointments, he has lunch with Philippe Rousselot, whom he hopes to enlist as director of photography for the film. Upon reading the screenplay and the storyboards, Rousselot is won over by the "laboratory" aspect that the production will require. And Annaud is fascinated by the prospect of having someone so experienced (*Diva, Emerald Forest, Hope and Glory, Dangerous Liaisons*) direct the lighting of a motion picture filmed entirely in the open.

The head cameraman thinks about production matters, the director about lighting. Both men were made to work with each other.

Pierre Grunstein and Xavier Castano count the days left before the release of *The Name of the Rose* and, therefore, before their director becomes available.

Finally, on December 17, 170 theaters in France premier *The Name of the Rose.* In keeping with the tradition of releasing films on Wednesdays, Jean-Jacques Annaud spends the evening with his distributor. At midnight, the exact number of tickets is 24,483 for the Paris region, the best number of the day. Everyone explodes with joy. The next day, the director grants his last interviews and leaves for a fifteen-day rest in Sri Lanka.

On Christmas Eve, Pierre Grunstein sends Claude Berri the estimate for the film: $22 million.

A fatalist at heart, the producer acquiesces, hoping that this figure will not be exceeded but all the while knowing that, for a film such as this one, unbudgeted costs are inevitable.

The adventure has just begun.

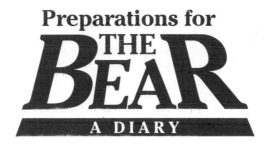

Preparations for THE BEAR
A DIARY

Shooting is set to begin on Monday, May 18, 1987. Claude Berri, Jean-Jacques Annaud, the Renn Productions crew, animation specialists, scientific advisors, American animal trainers, and special-effects personnel have only four and a half months—exactly 137 days—to complete this gigantic operation. Claude Berri hasn't wavered in five years. He is absolutely committed to this crazy project. His conviction rests on one idea, on one filmscript, and essentially on one man—Jean-Jacques Annaud—for whom nothing is impossible.

Friday, January 2

Annaud has just returned from Sri Lanka. A meeting is held at Claude Berri's home with Pierre Grunstein and Xavier Castano. They decide to send £265,000 to Jim Henson's studio in London so that the specialists there can start manufacturing the animatronics. At Renn Productions' offices, Jacques Allaire is visited by a man named Dieter Kraml. Weighing two hundred pounds, this iron-fisted German trainer is famous for his wonderful animals and for his light touch as a trainer. He is currently raising bears and owns a pair of female twins. The animal manager keeps Dieter in mind while thinking of Youk's mother.

Monday, January 5

Annaud leaves for the Auvergne to scout a location for a commercial film that has just been assigned him. The associate producer and the first assistant are sorry to see that the director has escaped them once again.

At the Vincennes zoo, the mood is jovial. Two bear cubs are born; they are known as necklace bears, because of the Y-shaped white streak that stands out on their dark chests. At night, François Hugues and Maryvonne Leclerc-Cassan retrieve the two cubs, which their mother has abandoned, and immediately convey them to a room heated to 77 degrees, where two incubators lined with straw are awaiting them. Bundled up in blankets and tucked between hot-water bottles, the cubs are fast asleep in their new home.

Tuesday, January 6

Grunstein flies to Prague. He has arranged to meet the head of the largest circus in Czechoslovakia, the Umberto Circus, which is reputed to have a number of extremely well trained brown bears. After three hours of talks, however, the answer is negative. The circus is unable to part with its bears because it has already committed them for a summer tour in Russia. Pierre asks the president of Filmexport in Prague and Milos Forman, a twenty-year associate of Claude Berri, to intercede on his behalf. Together, they manage to persuade the head of the circus to lend the movie the bears on the condition that Grunstein provide the circus with a substitute performance for its summer tour. Thus, the associate producer is suddenly turned into a circus booking agent. He contacts several circus companies in Europe, comes up with a panther act, and returns to Paris reassured.

Wednesday, January 7

Grunstein nearly chokes when he receives the proposed contract from the American trainer Doug Seus. Bart's salary has doubled. The American trainer also wants his wife, Lynne, as well as their children, his son-in-law, Clint, and another trainer to join him on location. Bart's food (carrots, potatoes, red meat), beverages, sweets (doughnuts, cakes, marshmallows) have to be imported from the United States. Salmon, which Bart adores, will be imported from Canada. And, as soon as the bear arrives in Europe, the producers will be in charge of providing Bart's chicken, at the rate of fifteen every day. Bart eats only raw, boned chicken. The producers will have to pay for two twenty-one-square-foot freezers for food storage. The producers will also have to rent a plane capable of transporting two twenty-seven-foot-long trailer trucks, one to carry the bear, the other to carry food and materials.

Faced with demands that only the most temperamental movie star could make, the associate producer replies with a counterproposal. He understands that it would be nice for family members to accompany the trainers, but says that the producers can take only the three individuals necessary for the upkeep of the bear. The producers will pay for Bart's food and for the freezers, but they will buy provisions on location. As for the trailer trucks, since these are useless on narrow mountain roads, the producers will build one or more vehicles necessary for the transportation of the bear and other materials.

Friday, January 9

Home from a night of scouting, Annaud is awakened by a telephone call from the Vincennes zoo. The two "necklace" cubs born on January 5 have just died due to pulmonary congestion resulting from an electrical malfunction occasioned by a general strike. In spite of hot-water bottles, blankets, and the care of veterinarians, the cubs were unable to survive the cold at night.

However, a brown bear has just been born. As soon as it is abandoned by its mother, the doctors retrieve it and place it in a small incubator.

Saturday, January 10

From Orly Airport at 8:20 A.M., Annaud and Xavier Castano leave for Lisbon. The Czech bears that Pierre Grunstein saw in Prague are touring Portugal. The director is disappointed. They may be well trained, but they are too glum and skinny.

Sunday, January 11

From Lisbon, Jean-Jacques and Xavier fly to London. Their destination is Jim Henson's Creature Shop.

The studio is managed by Chris Carr and John Stephenson, the inventor of the animatronic monkey for the movie *Max mon amour*. They debate the number of actors needed to mimic a bear. Jean-Jacques thinks that, for the roles of Kaar and Iskwao, one actor would not be big enough to look like an

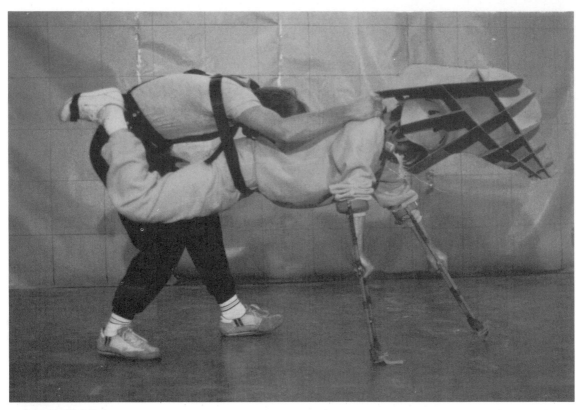

January 11, 1987. At Jim Henson's Creature Shop in London, actors experiment with how best to simulate a bear.

adult bear; two actors will be needed beneath the bearskin. The British find this concept too cumbersome. Training would take a long time and the positions required of both actors would be impossible. The actor placed in the rear would have to bear the weight of the actor in the front and wouldn't be able to carry that weight for more than three minutes at a stretch. Reluctantly, Jean-Jacques goes along with the majority opinion. One actor per bear, then.

Monday, January 12

Jean-Jacques meets Philippe Rousselot, who has been hired as director of photography for an upcoming commercial, to go over some of the shots. Meanwhile, Claude Berri flies to Munich to see Bernd Eichinger, the German producer and distributor of *The Name of the Rose*, who wants to buy the German rights to *The Bear*. Berri won't commit himself. Before signing any contracts with European distributors, he must first go to the United States, where a major distributor has made an attractive offer. Pierre Grunstein and

Xavier Castano have lunch together. Xavier is inexhaustible when it comes to bears. For a month he has been poring over every specialized work on bears, and he now knows how to tell a Baribal from a brown bear, a grizzly from a Kodiak. He plunges into *The Guide to Animal Traces*, which shows pictures of bear droppings and tracks.

Thursday, January 15

To organize the dog pack, Jacques Allaire contacts André Noël, who is considered one of the world's best trainers of attack dogs. The producer hasn't decided on the breed of the dogs yet. All he has in mind is a pack of ten dogs, all of them unleashed, with foaming, bloodied mouths, accompanied by a gentle and affectionate Airedale.

As for the other animals—stags, eagles, deer, horses, mules, lynxes, tortoises, trout, owls—the animal manager is contacting all of the major European specialists in animal procurement, as well as a German animal agent who has an impressive catalog of all the owners of trained animals in Europe. In the Auvergne, Annaud is filming his commercial. The snow is four feet deep and the temperature is five degrees.

Friday, January 16

Claude Berri has just landed in Los Angeles. He has an appointment with the executives of one of the largest American film studios. As always, for financial matters, he is accompanied by Paul Rassam. Rassam is the most hard-driving negotiator in Renn Productions. For many years, he has been on such excellent terms with directors like John Boorman, Milos Forman, Michael Cimino, Philipp Kauffman, Roland Joffe, and Francis Ford Coppola that he has always been able to undercut his competition in order to distribute their films in France. To release *The Bear* in the United States, the American studio makes an offer of $7.5 million. But the conditions are such that even if the movie were successful, Berri would be left with little else than his eyes to cry with. The president of the film studio then makes another proposal: to produce *The Bear* jointly. However, he feels the estimates are much too high. He would like Annaud and Grunstein to spend three weeks at his office revising their estimate. If the director refuses to go along with the proposed cuts, then they will simply have to get another director. Berri stands up. His partnership with the American studio has lasted two and a half minutes.

Saturday, January 17

Annaud and Philippe Rousselot return from the Auvergne.

Pierre Grunstein and Xavier Castano are relieved to meet their director. He has an appointment with Noëlle Boisson. She has edited more than a hundred commercials for him; she has also edited his film *Hothead*. She was unable to accept the offer to edit *Quest for Fire*, because editing was being handled in London and she was unable to go there. For *The Name of the Rose*, the fiancée of the producer was an editor. Conflicts now seem unavoidable. But Jean-Jacques Annaud is obstinate and loyal. He has a high regard for Noëlle Boisson. She will edit *The Bear*.

Tuesday, January 20

Jacques Allaire flies to Hannover to visit the German trainer Dieter Kraml, whom he met in Paris earlier in January. His twins are just right to play Youk's mother. Back in Paris, Jacques shares his thoughts with Jean-Jacques Annaud, who will be going to Germany himself over the weekend. The director hopes his animal manager will be able to locate a tame mother bear with a cub to play the scenes depicting the love between Youk and his mother.

Thursday, January 22

Another departure for London, at 8:30 A.M. It is imperative that Jean-Jacques and Xavier visit the special-effects studio once a week to better monitor the evolution of the animatronics. In the studio, they find Ailsa Berk teaching gymnastics to a group of men who don't appear to be professional mimes or dancers. Most of them are clumsy and flabby. A cameraman is videotaping them. Once the training session is over, John Stephenson gathers everyone— about thirty in all—and explains the subject of the film, and then plays a videocassette showing the habits of bears in a London zoo.

The mimes who have been selected will begin rehearsing early in February and will be hired for the duration of the filming, till the end of September— twenty-eight weeks in all.

While Ailsa Berk begins casting, Jean-Jacques and Xavier shut themselves up in an office on the second floor that is messy beyond description. After dusting off a corner of the table, Annaud opens up his storyboards and reads out:

"*Artificial flowers, yellow pollen.* It may look easy on paper, but for the flowers to fall at the right moment, we have to insert tiny air sacs in each stem that will burst and release powder. Campanulas. That would be nice, don't you think?"

"Or maybe an electromagnetic system," adds Xavier.

Jean-Jacques continues reading: "*After digesting wild strawberries, Youk . . .* We're all agreed on wild strawberries, right? However, we'll use the fake cub. We also have to think about dew on the fruit and be particularly careful about the lighting. These strawberries are a real pain. Let's move on to the frog. Do we have a mechanical frog?"

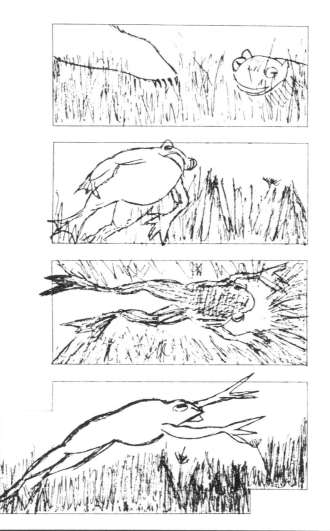

Sketches from the storyboards outline serious production problems.

Xavier: "No. Because Jean-Philippe Varin thinks we can pull it off with a real frog."

Jean-Jacques: "O.K. But I want its chest to swell. I still don't see how we'll be able to have both the cub and the frog in the same frame. No, we have to use a plastic frog, the kind that is found in toy stores. I could make it a humorous frog that will surprise Youk.

"Let's move on: *Youk lies on the grass.* We'll have to store grass, in case we have to replace it if the cub begins tearing it out."

Xavier: *"The frog takes a huge and sudden leap."*

Jean-Jacques: "You see, it's absolutely necessary to have a fake frog and a real cub.

"*The frightened faces of the hunters. Tom and Bill stooping over bear droppings.* Droppings, have you got that taken care of? *Weird-shaped clouds.* There are wonderfully shaped clouds in Germany and Austria, when the sun sets above the crags. We'll see about that with Rousselot. *Youk's dream. A hairy frog followed by a smaller one leap in slow motion.* That has to be done in the studio, and we'll let fantasy guide us. We must absolutely find a way to create the dream sequences."

Xavier: "What if we used divers dressed as frogs and had them leap about in a swimming pool surrounded by unusual vegetation?"

Jean-Jacques: "The swimming-pool liquid might have to be as thick as oil. Think of controlling the light both in the sky and in the water. Why not ask Ailsa Berk and a child to be the divers? We could set up trampolines behind the scenes from which they jump into the water."

Once Ailsa Berk has finished casting, Jean-Jacques and Xavier step into the staff room to watch the takes. None of the mimes is the right size to play Kaar's part. Most are no good. Some, trying to be more convincing as bears, think it clever to emit loud shouts. The filmmaker is annoyed. He has the feeling things are not progressing. It's one of those typical preliminary production days during which one thinks that something is bound to happen but nothing does.

Fortunately, the production of the fake animals is progressing well. An artist is sculpting the shapes of a nose, a mouth, and eyes on a clay model of a bear's head that will serve as the casting mold for Kaar. Another artist is designing Youk's body. Jean-Jacques suggests that he should widen Youk's head and neck to stress the cub's babyish appearance.

Friday, January 23

The animal trainer, Jacques Allaire, and André Noël, the dog trainer, travel ninety miles from Paris to visit Madame de Rothschild, who owns a pack of eighty Rottweilers. She knows each by name. However, none of them knows how to imitate attacking. Jacques and André then go to take a look at imposing mastiffs, but none of them knows how to jump.

In the evening, Claude Berri and Paul Rassam return from Los Angeles without having signed a contract. The financial success of *Jean de Florette* and *Manon of the Spring* allows Claude Berri to hold out for the best offer.

Saturday, January 24

Annaud and Xavier Castano fly to Hannover. They visit Dieter Kraml, whom Jacques Allaire had visited four days before.

In a cage, the female twins sit patiently. Their coats are ruddy beige and their faces are haloed in bronze-hued fur. They're gracious and meek. Their claws, which are of a rare and spotless white, are as long as manicured fingernails. The director would gladly book one of them to play the role of Youk's mother. But the trainer will hear none of it. Twins should never be separated—heaven forbid! Jean-Jacques signs up both.

January 20, 1987. These twins, owned by trainer Dieter Kraml, are signed up to play Youk's mother.

Monday, January 26

Annaud and Philippe Rousselot have a meeting in the production offices. Together they define the scenery, drawing their inspiration from such Romantic painters as Caspar David Friedrich and Albert Bierstadt. They discuss the crew. They also decide to use a wide-angle format and to use three cameras to have a variety of shots.

Tuesday, January 27

In the Bois de Boulogne, Jean-Jacques Annaud, Xavier Castano, and Jacques Allaire meet André Noël to cast the dogs. After testing various breeds, the trainer has settled on six: a herding dog, a German shepherd, a Flemish drover, a working breed from Picardy, a Doberman pinscher, and an Airedale. Taking turns, each dog lunges and attacks André Noël. Jean-Jacques doesn't take long to decide. He is impressed by the power, the carriage, and the black coat of the Doberman pinscher, even though the trainer is partial to the shepherd (shepherds are most trainers' unrivaled favorites). The director also adds the curly-haired, blond Airedale with a sweet face to the pack.

In the afternoon, Xavier calls Ailsa Berk. She has been scouring the greater London area for human giants to play Kaar's role but has had no luck at all.

Worried, the first assistant asks a French casting agency to launch a search in circuses, theaters, and universities, as well as in shoe stores, starting with size 16, and stores selling clothing for tall men.

Wednesday, January 28

In Paris, that night, a man named Baldwyn receives a telephone call. Originally from Normandy, he has been studying theater since 1983 at the University, and has been taking dancing, speech, and movement courses. But if his telephone is ringing tonight it's because he is six feet eight inches tall. Xavier Castano asks him to fly with Jean-Jacques Annaud to London to meet Ailsa Berk.

Thursday, January 29

At the Vincennes zoo, Xavier and Jacques Allaire visit the small brown cub which was born on January 9. Of course, they call it Youk. The twenty-day-old cub is comfortably sheltered between two hot-water bottles in an incubator at the veterinarians' offices.

The cub is six inches tall and weighs fourteen ounces. At two months, he will measure sixteen inches and weigh six pounds. At the time of filming, he will measure thirty inches and weigh twenty-two to twenty-six pounds. In two years he will be six feet tall and weigh 550 pounds.

He has no teeth, his eyes are still closed and his ear ducts still clogged, and his tongue is out of proportion to his overall size. Only his claws are flawlessly shaped: they are already hard and pointed. At birth, he was miraculously saved. Just after he was born, his mother picked him up in her mouth and dropped him. At that precise moment the two vets rushed to his rescue.

It is now 4:30 P.M. Youk is hungry and emits shrieks that are as piercing as those of a newborn baby. One of the vets takes him on his knees and feeds him from a baby bottle. A five-inch syringe filled with dog's milk is attached to a plastic nipple.

Youk has six baby bottles per day. And he'll do so for two months.

Every day, the doctors tend to the wounds his mother inflicted on him. They regret not having known the precise needs of the film in the spring of 1986. The previous year had been so productive that, during the rutting period in the spring of 1986, the doctors felt compelled to separate the males from the females to limit the number of births.

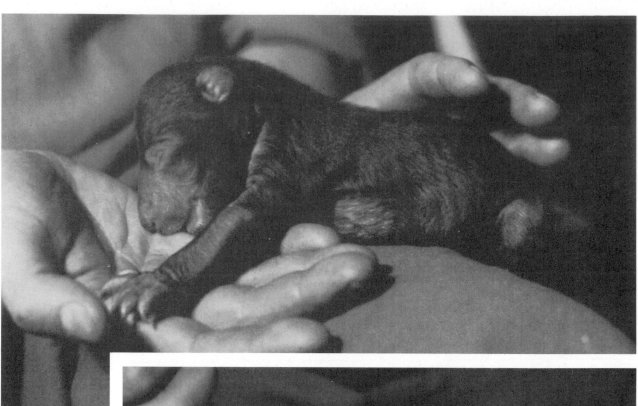

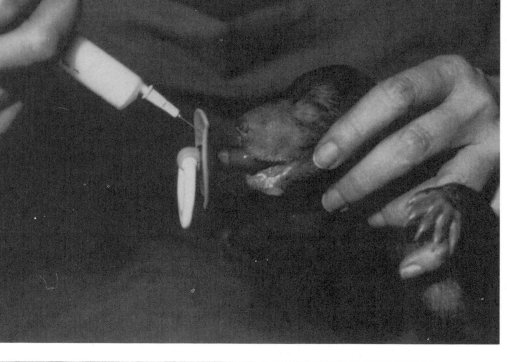

January 29, 1987. A twenty-day-old brown bear cub, measuring six inches in length and weighing fourteen ounces.

The newborn cub is fed milk six times a day.

Friday, January 30

Annaud, Xavier Castano, and Baldwyn take the 8:30 A.M. flight to London.

Because the manufacturing of the animatronics has completely taken over the studio, there is no space for rehearsing. Ailsa Berk has requisitioned a secularized church not more than one hundred feet away. Michael Cuckson, one of the mimes she recruited the day before, is a six-foot nine-inch giant who has captured Jean-Jacques's attention. He is fearsome. Baldwyn auditions and proves talented and resourceful, though somewhat stiff. None of the other average-sized mimes auditioning for the role of Iskwao satisfy Jean-Jacques. He suggests that Ailsa Berk play Youk's mother, in addition to her role as coordinator. She will continue looking for more actors.

Monday, February 2

Annaud has invited Xavier Castano to work with him at his mill in France. He had fallen in love with the mill at first sight and purchased it fifteen years before. On three peaceful acres of meadows, sheep and ewes are grazing, and rabbits, fleeing hunters, come to seek asylum.

His favorite room is on the first floor. Along the shelves of his huge library, his books are arranged with care. There are scientific and ethological books, encyclopedias, dictionaries, art books, a complete catalog of all the churches in France. On the mantelpiece, he has arranged a wonderful collection of antique cameras. In front of the fireplace, discreetly stacked, are trophies he was awarded for his commercials; his two Césars for best film and best directing for *Quest for Fire;* and his Oscar for *Black and White in Color.*

With his first assistant, he goes over the storyboards, reexamining each sketch, and finds ways around problems. Before each scene, however, the first reaction is always the same: "It's going to be extremely difficult."

At the Vincennes zoo, the vets, François Hugues and Maryvonne Leclerc-Cassan, are very worried. The wounds sustained by the cub are festering again. They spend their entire weekend caring for the cub.

Tuesday, February 3

Annaud and Xavier Castano visit the Zoo des Dômes, near Clermont-Ferrand, to meet the owner, Madame Sauvadet. The reception is cool, distant, even aggressive. With wary eyes, the energetic woman prowls around her visitors like a creature on the watch. The answer is no. No, her lynx will not be filmed in Germany or Austria. Yes, Annaud may look at the animal, but the lynx will not leave the zoo. She has raised him from birth. He is now four years old and measures almost three feet. He's a wonderful creature but too small for the scene in which he would pursue the bear cub.

Madame Sauvadet takes them to see two tame pumas whose larger size is better for the confrontation scene. In Jean-Jacques's mind, the change from lynx to puma has already taken place.

Gradually the mistrust begins to fade. Madame Sauvadet is forty-five years old. She is one of those rare people in Europe who breed wild animals to return them to their natural habitat. In 1983, she was raising four bear cubs who were giving her a lot of trouble. Whenever the telephone rang, all four practical jokers would spring into action by stealing food from the refrigerator, squeezing toothpaste tubes, or climbing into the bathtub. On a day when several journalists came to visit, the bears suddenly disappeared. She and the journalists searched high and low, but in vain. After the journalists left, she found the bears in her bed, hiding beneath the sheets, "giggling like mad."

Three other bear cubs had just been born in her zoo. The film director asks Madame Sauvadet whether she will agree to train them before filming begins. Triplets! That would be too much work. But to compensate for her refusal, she agrees to entrust the bears to the production.

At Vincennes, ninety-nine hours after his wounds started festering, and in spite of the tireless care of doctors, the little cub has died. The autopsy reveals internal injuries due to postpartum trauma. The zoo expects no more births. But the doctors have not abandoned the film. They will care for cubs from other zoos and will provide medical supervision on the set.

Thursday, February 5

It's 7:45 A.M. Jean-Jacques, Xavier, the animal manager, and the zoological advisor, Jean-Philippe Varin, fly from Paris to Munich. In Munich, an assistant awaits the French troupe. They climb into a minibus. Thirty-one miles southwest of Munich is the small hamlet of Kerschlach. It is ensconced in larch and privet forests and its low-lying farms surround a Benedictine monastery. Jean-Jacques smiles as he thinks of *The Name of the Rose*. The owner of one of these farms, Herr Nemitz, a very traditional Bavarian wearing velvet breeches and a feathered hat, shows off majestic black stallions, purchased the year before in Czechoslovakia. He also shows them a female Cheyenne horse and mules. His horses are handsome, much too handsome for hunters. Annaud is looking for animals that look more rustic. Herr Nemitz will survey neighboring farms later in the day. Before leaving, they take a pretzel-and-coffee break and then visit the ponds of Mühlen, which are filled with trout. Jean-Jacques needs trout for the fishing scene. He places an order for three hundred trout, each of which will have to weigh four pounds and measure twenty inches at the time of filming.

At 5 P.M. they return to Munich. In the minibus, Jean-Jacques, Xavier, and Varin aren't idle. They pore over the storyboards. Xavier tapes their conversation, as Jean-Jacques reads: "*A robin. I want a bird who'll sing the morning song.*"

Jean-Philippe: "I don't have a northern-Canadian singing bird, but I'll give you a cassette with sounds made by various singing birds. You can pick the one you want."

Jean-Jacques: "*Youk's fur is disheveled.* What do you suggest?"

Jean-Philippe: "Oh, that's easy. We'll put the cub in a stocking, like a woman's stocking, but made to fit his body, so that his fur will become somewhat matted. The moment you say, 'Start rolling,' we'll remove the stocking. Don't worry, the little bear's fur will look quite disheveled."

The road begins to wind. Everyone's reading speed gradually slackens. At the hotel, Jean-Jacques gives himself a half-hour to make telephone calls. He has acute telephonitis. On the road, at gas stations, between airplanes, in coffee shops, one of the most organized men in his profession always carries loose change and his international Telecom card.

During dinner, Jean-Philippe Varin begins telling animal stories. He is an inexhaustible storyteller, a fifty-volume self-contained encyclopedia. During a conversation, he might describe the macho behavior of kingfishers, the ability of crows who have nested near railway lines to mimic train whistles, the habitat of pumas, the ferocity of lynxes, the laziness of sea tortoises, or the eleven-foot leaps of black panthers.

Meanwhile, in California, Pierre Grunstein is speaking with Steve Martin, whom he hasn't seen since 1983. He gives him a copy of the storyboards so that Mark Wiener, the trainer, can start training his two bears, Doc and Grizz, before Jean-Jacques arrives at the end of February.

The bears are even handsomer than they were three years before. The associate producer asks Martin for a sample of fur as well as the measurements of both bears. The British crew is eagerly awaiting these measurements so as to match the animatronics to the sizes of real bears. Martin agrees to snip off a sample of the bears' fur but refuses to provide any measurements as long as the contract is not signed. His conditions are very reasonable.

Friday, February 6

At 7:30 A.M. in the lobby of the hotel in Munich, Jean-Jacques displays his double-soled boots, purchased in Canada; one sole hugs the foot, the other is made of woolen fiber. The minibus, which is headed for Innsbruck, stops at a wildlife preserve in Thannhausen that shelters ibexes, stags, and wild sheep. The preserve is managed by a stern-faced, tough-talking man who quotes prices before showing his animals. Jean-Jacques decides he does not want to deal with him. They return to Mr. Nemitz in Kerschlach. He has looked around the neighboring farms for other horses. Mr. Hoffman, who owns magnificent fir-wood stables, has two geldings; they are white, gentle, and disciplined, attractive, but almost too handsome. At another farm, managed by a ruddy-cheeked, thick-set, affable woman, the horses clearly look more rural. The director books two of them, one of which is a sprightly Dutch horse with white hooves that look like half-boots.

They return to Munich at around 4:30 P.M. In the heart of the downtown area a twenty-foot truck is parked. The minibus driver stops. The crew gathers around the rear of the truck, which stinks in the sweltering heat. Everyone is dumbstruck. The truck contains four giant tortoises, each measuring four feet. Carrots, potatoes, and rotten herbs litter the floor. The tortoises—the youngest is thirty-six years old, the oldest eighty-five—belong to a couple who have been touring the animal shows of Europe. Jean-Jacques bursts out laughing. One of the scenes in the movie has Youk playing with a tortoise. But these are at least three times the size of the cub. The minibus takes off again.

The next appointment is in room 122 at the Holiday Inn. As soon as they open the door, the visitors are greeted by a lynx coming out of the bathroom. The trainer, who has just arrived from Berlin, didn't know where to stay in the city. The lynx is a six-month-old male with a mischievous gaze. But he's too small. The trainer argues to the contrary. Jean-Jacques categorically refuses. The scene in which Youk must face the lynx would be ridiculous. Besides, in the director's mind, the lynx has already been displaced by a puma.

These scouting expeditions are very important. Even if they don't bring immediate results, they enable the crew to test different options and make last-minute changes. At any rate, over the years, Jean-Jacques has learned that he must check on everything.

Back at the hotel, Jean-Jacques meets Toni Ludi. Ludi was responsible for much of the scenery in *The Name of the Rose*. The filmmaker had appreciated his efficiency and initiative. He now asks him to be the production designer for *The Bear*. Ludi's job has two aspects: first he must inspect all of the present locations in detail; then he must develop a set design that matches exactly the natural scenery and can be rebuilt as many time as necessitated by damage caused by the animals. Ludi, who is a specialist in studio and interior designs, is delighted to have an opportunity to work out in the open.

Saturday, February 7

The group wakes up at 6:00 A.M. and leaves at 7:00 A.M. It is hailing, and the temperature has dropped below fifteen degrees. Headed for Riedenburg, near Nuremberg, the crew arrives an hour and a half later at a castle perched on top of a cliff. The place seems to be inhabited by large horned owls, barn owls, and wood owls. Poised majestically in a paddock is a lone vulture. Jean-Jacques knows vultures well. He used a vulture to model the features of Malachie, the ascetic-faced librarian in *The Name of the Rose*.

A royal eagle, guided by his trainer, flies up and lands on the crest of one of the turrets; then he flies back to his perch and is off flying again, finally diving down toward his master, who rewards him by tossing him day-old chicks that the bird swallows gluttonously. Jean-Jacques books the eagle, as well as an owl.

They leave at 10:00 A.M. The expedition has been successful. They take a last look at the storyboards while the minibus heads toward the airport. Jean-Philippe Varin is dozing; Xavier resists as best he can the numbness that gradually takes over. Tireless, Jean-Jacques hums and laughs. Varin and Allaire will be on their way to Paris; Jean-Jacques and Xavier will leave for London.

In the 747, the director and first assistant finish rereading the three hundred pages of long storyboards, a thick volume that has been leafed through and combed a hundred times; it has been soaked by rain and imbued with the odor of tobacco smoke from hotel bars and gas fumes from the minibus.

At Henson's Creature Shop, Ailsa Berk displays her new group of mimes.

February 7, 1989. In a park in London, the actors who will imitate the bears go through their daily training: Baldwyn, on the left, will play Kaar and Roman Stefanski will be Iskwao.

The director confirms her choices and completes the selection. Michael Cuckson, six feet nine inches tall, will play the part of Kaar, and Baldwyn, six feet eight inches, will be his understudy; Roman Stefanski will be the enticing Iskwao, and Ailsa Berk will play Youk's mother.

As soon as these decisions have been finalized, Jean-Jacques and Xavier head back to Paris.

Monday, February 9

Jacques Allaire has received good news about bear cubs. In the zoos of Peaugres, Nancy, Saint-Vrain, Munich, and Thoiry, Baribal and brown bear cubs have just been born.

Annaud has lunch with the director of Filmexport, from Prague, who is passing through Paris. In the movie, both Kaar and Youk have dreams. The film director plans to use animation techniques for these dream sequences, a technique in which Czech filmmakers excel (after the war, a handful of Czech filmmakers started a specialized animation studio within the state production studios). The camera would photograph puppets, shot after shot, so as to create movement. Annaud is thinking of movies made by Trnka, Čapek, Doubkova, Svankmajen, Barta, and Pojar, which he had seen at the Ciné-mathèque as a student. The director of Filmexport suggests that he arrange for Jean-Jacques to meet with the film directors and to view some of their films in Prague in March.

Tuesday, February 10

Still in the United States, Pierre Grunstein flies to Heber City, where the trainer Doug Seus lives. Since the counterproposal that Pierre submitted to him a month earlier, the animal tamer has shown no signs of life. As soon as Pierre arrives, Doug greets him with open arms. Before discussing the terms of the agreement, he suggests that they go and have a look at Bart. In three years, Bart has grown bigger and stronger, all the while remaining extremely talented. Pierre asks for a sample of Bart's fur as well as for his measurements, which the British crew needs. Doug agrees to provide the fur sample. As for the measurements, he'll give them only after the contract is signed. At lunch, they begin negotiating. Pierre offers to have a cage made to transport Bart. The trainer refuses. He wants Bart to travel in his usual trailer. Pierre tries to persuade him that the trailer is too large to fit in any airplane. Seus stands up, goes to take the measurements of the trailer, comes back, calls Lufthansa, and yields before the evidence: Grunstein is right. The next problem: the trainer refuses to allow Bart to travel on the same airplane as Doc and Grizz, Steve Martin's bears! Without fully understanding Seus's reasons for this, Grunstein promises that Bart will travel on a separate flight.

Back in France, the associate producer goes over the budget. This is the most difficult estimate he has ever had to put together. The cost of special effects and of the dream sequences remains unknown. And the scenery too is a tricky question. When one reads the film script, everything seems so simple. But to tame nature is an entirely different story. While waiting, he juggles English pounds, German marks, Austrian schillings, American dollars, French francs.

Thursday, February 12

Sitting at his desk, Xavier Castano is having the same worries as Pierre Grunstein. He has just begun to listen to his taped conversations with Jean-Jacques Annaud so as to establish a shooting schedule. How much time will a bear need to play a scene? How many hours will a trainer need to set up safety wires between the animals and the crew? How many days will the set designers need to create artificial rocks and grass, or to plant trees, flowers, and shrubs? He asks himself dozens of unanswerable questions.

The building of the fake rocks turns into a headache, requiring three weeks for completion. They have to be light enough to be carried easily, but resilient enough to withstand the bears' claws.

Friday, February 13

Some very bad news. The English mime Michael Cuckson, who is supposed to play Kaar's role, has just undergone a physical examination and his physiotherapist has noticed lesions on his spinal cord. The mime is forbidden to carry any loads whatsoever. Thoroughly dismayed, Xavier suggests to Ailsa Berk that she have his understudy, Baldwyn, replace him. But the coordinator is not terribly enthusiastic. She would prefer that the special-effects team remain entirely British.

Monday, February 16

Xavier Castano has had a horrible weekend before giving the bad news to Jean-Jacques Annaud. But the latter regards obstacles as normal steps to be overcome during the preparation of a film. After another casting call in London, Ailsa Berk has selected Michael Blair, a six-foot-nine-inch-tall dancer who has neither the talent nor the instincts of his predecessor, but who, on the other hand, has been given a far cleaner bill of health.

Thursday, February 19

Ailsa Berk spends the day in Paris reviewing Baldwyn's progress. Won over, she calls Xavier with her decision: Baldwyn will be the mime for Kaar, and Michael Blair his understudy. The Frenchman, who is in seventh heaven, thinks it indeed ironic that, six years earlier, a military doctor turned him down as physically unfit for duty.

Friday, February 20

In a Belgian zoo, a female Kodiak has recently foaled. Annaud has been eagerly awaiting such an event, for he wants to observe the relationship between a mother bear and her cub.

Mr. Wauter, the head of the zoo, is an original. After having made a fortune in real estate, he invested everything he had to acquire animals for the zoo. Six months ago, while walking by the bear enclosure with his dog, he realized, too late, that one of the gates was not properly locked. A Kodiak suddenly seized his dog by the neck. Mr. Wauter attempted to rescue his dog but was himself attacked. All of his ribs were broken and an arm and a leg were mauled.

Jean-Jacques Annaud explains his problem. Would it be possible to film in the zoo? Would it be necessary to dig a trench at the site to move the Kodiak and her cub? Mr. Wauter can't believe his ears. These men are crazier than he is. They have come all the way from Paris for only a few minutes of film. He bursts out laughing and asks whether the production is subsidized. Jean-Jacques is overjoyed.

Saturday, February 21

Toni Ludi visits Paris. Together with Annaud, he reviews the storyboards with an eye toward building the sets. In the mountains, vegetation has a tendency to change its color and other qualities in the space of a very few days. They have to incorporate artificial elements into the natural setting while keeping the natural look. Ludi plans to use a very resilient material to replace the vegetation that will gradually perish under the feet of 180 people and, of course, the passage of bears.

That afternoon, Jean-Jacques explains to Corinne Jorry, the head costume designer, that he wants the hunters to be clothed in the style of the 1880s. Such clothes are unavailable in France. There are still antique-clothing stores in Montreal. The designer will fly there in the next few days.

Sunday, February 22

At his mill, Jean-Jacques Annaud packs. His destinations are London, and then the United States. Claude Berri calls him:

"When you arrive in Los Angeles, get in touch with film-studio executives whom you know. I'm relying on you to win them over, but without firing them up. If you seduce them too well, they'll want to play a bigger role during production. But I don't want to give up anything, except for the distribution."

Annaud hangs up feeling perplexed. To seduce without seducing is the one thing he doesn't know how to do.

Monday, February 23

In the taxi on the way to Henson's studio in London, Annaud, who is accompanied by Castano and Grunstein, does not waste a second. With his Filofax on his knees, he neatly recopies the addresses of London bookstores where he has shopped. He wants to get some books about animal behavior. He's a fanatical note-taker. His Filofax is a self-contained information center. Every city is allotted its own section: pages with restaurants, hotels, bookstores, other shops, museums, each marked with symbols, as in a guidebook, but the marks are not forks, stars, or castles, simply hearts.

The studio is brimming with activity. Annaud thinks that the fake-fur samples are too beautiful. With the hairdressers, he decides that the skin should have more texture, more irregularities. In real life, bears get injured and ruin their

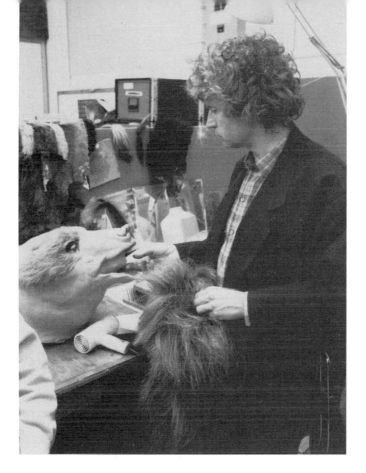

fur. Farther off, there are two plaster models. One seems to be for Baldwyn, the other for Ailsa Berk. With an electric kitchen knife, the costume designers cut through six inches of foam, which they then apply to the models. Once placed, the foam is held by a series of hoops made of large plastic slats that are flexible and secure. The foam and the hoops are then covered with a shiny, resilient brown cloth and sewn with cross-stitches. In three hours the carapace is finished.

Jean-Jacques is pleased with the work. Kaar's latex head is completed. The director asks that his eyes be enlarged, so as to give them greater expression, and that the nose, which looks more like a pig's than a bear's, be shortened. To convince the sculptor, the film director grimaces and twists his face around, struggling to imitate a bear as best he can.

Toward the end of the morning, a bearded, gray-haired, gray-eyed man arrives: Jim Henson himself. He has come from the United States especially to choose the puppeteers. In spite of the cold weather that infiltrates the secularized church, he has asked that the electric radiators be turned off. Their noise would disrupt the puppeteers' concentration. The twenty candidates take turns in front of the video camera in teams of four. One of them thrusts his arms inside a hairy life-sized koala bear's head while his partner manages the front paws with the help of controls. Close by, a second puppeteer activates a hairy brown dog. The latter is more sophisticated than the koala. Wires run the whole length of his skin and are connected to his eyes. The puppeteer's teammate fastens a belt around his partner's hips and, by radio, activates the wires to the dog's eyes.

Brian Henson, Jim's son, who is also a puppeteer, gives the go-ahead. Suddenly, the face is animated, first with worry, then with sadness, happiness, fear, surprise. Each expression has an uncanny realism. Brian Henson asks the puppeteers to play the scene together. The koala and the dog kiss each other, yawn, and nibble and caress each other. The dog places his head on the koala's shoulder. The koala bites Brian's finger, then seizes one of the dog's paws as the dog scowls at him. The scene is irresistible.

Xavier is fascinated. His eyes travel back and forth between the video screen and the shaggy animals as if he were watching a Punch and Judy show. Xavier's smile is infectious, and now Jean-Jacques too is smiling. He is delighted that his assistant has taken to the project. Jim Henson has followed everything with great attention. He never interferes, but his experience will dictate the best and final choice.

Once the casting is finished, Jean-Jacques takes an hour to rummage through the old bookshops of Cecil Beaton Street. He finds what he was looking for: works on the life of bears, their sexual behavior, the relationship between mother and cub. His reading is bound to generate some ideas for the scenes between Kaar and Iskwao, Kaar and Youk, Youk and his mother. While Pierre Grunstein and Xavier Castano head back to Paris, Jean-Jacques spends the night at Duke's Hotel. He has dinner delivered to his room, and, glad to be able to spend a peaceful evening alone, begins reading a book on animal sexuality.

Wednesday, February 25

Annaud leaves for Los Angeles. When he arrives, he checks in at the Beverly Hills Hotel, rents a red Mustang convertible, dines with his casting director, and goes over some of the research to be done concerning the characters of the two hunters and the dog handler.

Thursday, February 26

Still concerned about how to produce the dream sequences, Jean-Jacques contacts a company in Los Angeles that specializes in manufacturing and transforming colors. It is very well equipped and could do whatever he would require, but at an exorbitant price.

In the evening, he has dinner at the house of Sean Connery, the star of *The Name of the Rose*. The movie has been nominated for a César as Best Foreign Film. At Jean-Jacques's request, Connery will come to Paris for the ceremony.

Friday, February 27

Annaud goes to visit Steve Martin. He needs to discuss things with Mark Wiener, the trainer for Doc and Grizz. Together they go through the storyboards, sketch after sketch. Jean-Jacques asks many questions about whether what is written can actually be realized on film. Wiener's answers are technical in nature and to the point.

Saturday, February 28

Claude Berri and Paul Rassam land in Los Angeles, where they have an appointment at a film studio. For the second time, the offers they are made are unsatisfactory, and they decline.

Monday, March 2

Berri and Rassam have a meeting with the president of another film studio. Like his competitors, he is very excited by the project. Annaud is a rarity among European film directors: with only four films to his credit, he is known on the American continent. *Black and White in Color* won the Oscar for Best Foreign Film, Fox distributed *Quest for Fire* and co-produced *The Name of the Rose*. But the subjects of his films have always aroused suspicion. Upon hearing about the prehistoric film that had no script, studio executives would invariably ask the same question: "In what language will it be?"

The same thing had happened with his medieval detective story. A shudder ran down the corridors of the executive offices: "The fourteenth century? What religion is it?"

This time it's no different. *The Bear* remains a puzzle. "Five minutes of dialogue? Are you sure you'll be able to captivate an audience for an hour and a half with a film about the actions and emotions of an enormous Kodiak and a small cub?"

Though perplexed, the American film executives sense that this film might well be a blockbuster. But they are hard-bargaining businessmen. Since their conditions do not suit the French producers, Claude Berri keeps his *Bear* all to himself and returns to Paris.

Tuesday, March 3

The production and creative supervisors for the animatronics leave London and go to Belgium to visit the Kodiak and her cub, which Jean-Jacques had seen two weeks before. The Englishmen, who know the bears only through pictures, discover real animals. Their features, their eyes, their mouths, their gait will be invaluable in the manufacture of the animatronics.

Wednesday, March 4

During the next few days, a delicate operation awaits Jacques Allaire and the veterinarians François Hugues and Maryvonne Leclerc-Cassan: they must get the bear cubs. All of them are eight to ten weeks old, which is the ideal time for taking them and giving them to Jean-Philippe Varin until filming starts.

In the bear enclosure at the Thoiry zoo, the vets discover lairs dug at the foot of trees, between the roots, from which the cubs are heard crying. With no trouble at all, veterinarian Hugues catches the two Baribal cubs, places them in a box containing straw, hot-water bottles, and blankets, and whisks them away to the back of his car.

They are headed for Saint-Vrain, north of Paris. Here the situation is quite simple, for the bears live in cages. The zoo's head trainer separates the mother's cage from that of the three cubs. Another set of boxes, and they are back on the road toward Sainte-Montaine in the Sologne. On his property, Jean-Philippe Varin has installed a series of small cages in a thousand-square-foot space. As soon as the cubs arrive, the caretakers teach them how to drink from baby bottles. At the first feeding it takes them forty-five minutes to finish a bottle. By the third feeding, however, the cubs understand the trick; it even becomes necessary to tear the nipple from their mouths lest they suffocate between gulps. The caretakers stay up most of the night. The last bottle is at midnight, the first at six.

Thursday, March 5

Allaire and the veterinarians leave Sainte-Montaine for the Peaugres zoo, in the Ardèche. When they arrive, they are greatly disappointed. They had expected to find three brown cubs and two Baribals. Unfortunately, the lair of the brown bear was flooded. While she was moving, her three cubs were devoured by other bears. François Hugues takes the two Baribal cubs and bundles them up in two boxes. They return to Sainte-Montaine. In only twenty-four hours the cubs have become more boisterous and spirited. They nibble at anything that moves with their small, pointed teeth.

Saturday, March 7

Allaire and the vets return to Paris. They leave the seven cubs with Varin. The zoological advisor hires three neighborhood women to take care of the cubs.

Jean-Jacques arrives back in France. As soon as he lands, puts on his tuxedo and heads for the Hôtel Plaza to meet Sean Connery, who accompanies him to the Césars ceremony. Even after twenty-four hours of flying, the director looks well. He never experiences jet lag. After *Quest for Fire* (which was awarded two Césars, for Best Film and Best Director), will the movie people recognize *The Name of the Rose*? No one knows. Ornella Muti comes onstage to present the award for Best Foreign Film. The five nominees are *Hannah and Her Sisters* by Woody Allen, *The Mission* by Roland Joffé, *After Hours* by Martin Scorsese, *Out of Africa* by Sidney Pollack, and *The Name of the Rose* by Jean-Jacques Annaud.

Ornella Muti opens the envelope. The winner is . . . *The Name of the Rose*. Jean-Jacques, seated in the third row, rushes onto the stage and says, "The stranger is I." He beckons to Sean Connery and, with a gesture of rare elegance, offers him his César. The actor throws himself into the arms of his film director, who rushes out through the wings, pursued by a pack of journalists. He grants them forty-five minutes in the press room before returning to his seat. A few hours later, exhausted, he heads for his mill in Loiret. He hasn't really slept in thirty-six hours.

Monday, March 9

After lunching at Matignon as Prime Minister Jacques Chirac's guest, Jean-Jacques spends the afternoon at the Ministry Environment with Pierre Grunstein, Xavier Castano, Jacques Allaire, and Jean-Philippe Varin. Seated at the table are officials of the ministry, of the Central Committee for the Protection of Nature, the heads of the official Bear Group and of the Permanent National Council for the Protection of Nature, and experts on import/export problems. The producers have submitted a list of all the animals they intend to use in the making of the film. Jean-Jacques gives up the idea of using a robin and makes plans to find a substitute: the species is protected and is off-limits to filmmakers. The conversation turns to a commercial for which Varin tamed seagulls from the south of France for a commercial to be filmed in Brittany. One of the officials of the Permanent National Council for the Protection of Nature reproaches him for having damaged the reputation of Brittany's gulls.

They return to *The Bear*. Everyone present feels very positive about the project. Jean-Jacques obtains all the authorizations he requested, except for snails. It is forbidden to displace them from their natural environment. Naively, the director asks what happens when a snail is displaced from the garden to the kitchen. With all seriousness, the head of the Ministry of the Environment retorts that the answer lies with the Ministry of Agriculture.

Tuesday, March 10

A meeting is held at Renn Productions to discuss the situation regarding the animals. The bears who will portray Kaar and Iskwao and Youk's mother have been selected. As for the cubs, seven have already been selected, and five others will be obtained in the next few days. In addition, there are the two cubs of the twins owned by the German trainer Dieter Kraml that he will train until filming begins. In all there are fourteen cubs. Their number pleases Jean-Jacques.

With respect to the dogs, André Noël has contacted the association of Doberman pinscher trainers. He has selected ten that are already partially trained and has begun their specific training for the film. Given their pedigrees and the prizes they have won, Pierre Grunstein is forced to insure these dogs for a fortune. One of them, the European champion, is valued at $15,500, the others between $4,650 and $7,750.

After numerous inquiries, Jacques Allaire has booked five stags that belong to a large proprietor in Normandy. Jean-Jacques has decided to hire Madame Sauvadet's puma, and he also enlists Europe's most famous wild animal trainer, Thierry Leportier.

Wednesday, March 11

At the Dômes zoo, near Clermont-Ferrand, Jacques Allaire and François Hugues retrieve the three brown bear cubs cared for by Madame Sauvadet. Well propped up in a duffle bag, the three furry balls arrive in Paris in a sleeping car. Allaire tries to convince the conductor that he is bringing back home three puppies in need of love. Puzzled, the official asks if he can take a look inside the bag. But thanks to a good tip, he will be understanding until they arrive in Paris. The hours are long for the "nurses." Armed with a baby-bottle heater and dog's milk, they feed the cubs over and over. One cub is lying on his tummy, the other nibbles away at his neck, the third is on his chest. Jacques Allaire won't shut an eye all night long.

Thursday, March 12

Early in the morning, Maryvonne Leclerc-Cassan picks up François Hugues, Jacques Allaire, and the three cubs at the train station. With her are two brown cubs that the Nancy zoo had entrusted to the production the day before. They all leave for Sainte-Montaine, where the zoo is beginning to resemble a nursery.

Toward the end of the morning, Pierre Grunstein and Jean-Jacques Annaud leave for Prague, where they will meet the head of Filmexport. There they are shown a number of animated films. Jean-Jacques and Pierre are particularly interested in the films of Bretislav Pojar, a filmmaker now in his sixties who is a disciple of Trnka. They arrange to have dinner with him that same evening. Annaud explains the details of the dream sequences: the scene in which Youk, having eaten mushrooms, hallucinates that the mushrooms are transformed into butterflies, and the scene in which the cub dreams of a storm of frogs jumping into a red pond.

Pojar listens attentively and asks for a few weeks to consider whether he wants to participate.

Bretislav Pojar, the Czech animator, is selected to create the dream sequences.

Friday, March 13

While Pierre Grunstein becomes Jean-Jacques Annaud's guide to the enchanting city of Prague, which he is visiting for the first time, the actor Tchéky Karyo receives a telephone call in Paris from his agent about *The Bear*. Karyo has seen *Quest for Fire* and *The Name of the Rose*, and he ranks Jean-Jacques Annaud among the truly great film directors. He agrees to audition for the casting director the following week.

Monday, March 16

As soon as he is back in Paris, Jean-Jacques Annaud leaves for London with Xavier Castano and the mime Baldwyn. When he arrives at the studio, he shouts, "Hello, bears," but no one seems to notice him. They're all working too hard. Jean-Jacques is delighted with the way things are progressing.

Toward the end of the morning, he calls a meeting to determine the exact sequence of scenes in which the mechanical bears are to play their parts. Jean-Jacques begins to act out each scene, including the very first one—for the fun of it: he mimics the countryside, the wind, the sound of a river, the shriek of a bird. Right away, they discover a problem: how will the puppeteers conceal themselves when activating Youk? Trenches are suggested. Trenches? Xavier panics. He pictures bulldozers knocking down and chewing up the film set. He proposes, instead, that they erect a changeable structure that could serve as a rock or be covered with grass and flowers, and behind which the puppeteers would hide.

Jean-Jacques lingers over certain scenes that are especially complicated. For example: *Kaar seduces Iskwao*. The director asks Ailsa Berk to train the mime Roman Stefanski, who is to play the role of Iskwao, "as if he were rehearsing a number for the Crazy Horse Saloon": erotically and effeminately. On the other hand, Baldwyn, wearing Kaar's skin, will have to be macho, attempting to impress his future conquest by smashing everything standing in his way. To make sure everyone understands his plan, Jean-Jacques spends four hours acting out the emotions of the film: sadness, loneliness, anger, nonchalance, tenderness, and humor. He coughs, sniffles, yawns, snores, chews, and even licks John Stephenson. He knows, however, that today's sketchy outline will have to be adapted to real-life conditions on location.

Tuesday, March 17

Tchéky Karyo goes to the office of the casting director. Corinne Jorry, the costume designer, lends him a costume she brought back from Montreal. In front of the video camera, the casting director explains the role of the character. Tom, a hunter, has been living in the forest for several months with an older and more experienced fellow hunter. They are so busy hunting bears that they hardly talk to each other. In two minutes, Tchéky Karyo says that he already feels the role; he knows it "in his belly, on his back, everywhere." He tells

how he has built two houses with his father, insists that he is in perfect shape, talks about his relationship with nature, with objects. Exuberant, the actor finishes the test. On the spot, he decides to quit smoking, just like that, as if on a bet.

Wednesday, March 18

At Sainte-Montaine, Jacques Allaire and Xavier Castano are talking with Jean-Philippe Varin. The producers decide that it is necessary to separate the bear cubs until filming begins. If one of them were to fall ill, the eleven others would run the risk of becoming ill as well. The assistant director has already made the necessary contacts. A friend of François Hugues will take three cubs, and Madame Sauvadet has accepted to take one. Varin will keep the other eight. Every three days, the veterinarians will weigh them, check their teeth, and reevaluate their food. Because bear cubs grow very quickly, their food intake will have to be reassessed each week to make sure it keeps up with their growth.

Sonia Vandendries, one of the cubs' trainers, has been around bears her entire life.

Youk 1, an affectionate Baribal.

Youk 2, a sweet baby.

Youk 3, known as "Gogol," the Lilliputian of the bunch.

Youk 4, nicknamed "Zazou," a real whiner.

Youk 5, nicknamed "Bad Nicky," a mischievous devil.

Youk 6, called "Blackcurrant," with wary eyes.

Youk 7, nicknamed "Casserole Dish," extremely shy.

Youk 8, called "Kiwi," fearless.

Youk 9, nicknamed "Panda," as pretty as a picture.

Youk 10, called "Cadix," constantly looking for a caress.

Youk 11, nicknamed "Cadence," very cuddly.

Youk 12, named "Douce," independent and a bit aloof.

Monday, March 23

In Munich, bad news awaits Xavier Castano, who has come to settle some problems with Toni Ludi. The film set they had selected in Germany is buried under snow. The long-term weather forecast is disturbing. The snow probably won't be gone until June. Xavier is shattered. Ludi mentions a place called San Vigilio, in northern Italy, in the Dolomites, near Cortina d'Ampezzo, two hours from Venice. The first assistant director calls the director, who, as usual, receives the news with good cheer: "Let Toni Ludi start scouting in the Dolomites. I will join him in a few days."

Wednesday, March 25

Xavier leaves Munich and goes to Wiesbaden. At the center of an old army base, he meets Alfons Spindler. The man is illiterate but owns a luxurious Mercedes 500, twelve horses, six ponies, one elephant, two monkeys, three lamas, four pigs, twelve ducks, two dromedaries, one cow, three dogs, and, most important, one female adult bear and her two cubs. She is the only female bear in all of Europe who lives with her own offspring. Xavier wants to strike a deal right away. Alfons Spindler begins to panic. Usually his wife signs all the contracts, but today she is absent. He does understand numbers, however. On seeing the amount offered, Alfons signs the contract with an X.

Saturday, March 28

Jean-Jacques goes to visit the cubs at Sainte-Montaine. The director will meet his future stars for the first time.

In the nursery, each of the twelve cages is three feet long and two feet wide and is marked "Youk 1," "Youk 2," etc. School notebooks—purple for the Baribals, green for the brown bears—record the particulars of each bear: the date and place of birth, the date when the first tooth appeared, weight, size, the number of daily bottles, personality. In the middle of the room is a table that holds baby bottles, towels, and sponges. On the floor, a huge blanket serves as a play area, with bones and rubber balls. In the corner is "the droppery," a large sheet of cardboard on which are collected the daily droppings of each bear. If any sheet looks suspicious, it is immediately sent to the lab and analyzed. Everything is sterilized and impeccably clean.

When the crew arrives for the 11:00 A.M. bottle, pandemonium breaks loose in all the cages. The contents are swallowed in a few seconds. The casualties are as follows: Xavier's arm sustains a cut, Jean-Jacques's shirt is torn, and Pierre is scratched. The nurses have bite marks all over their necks and wrists. After feeding, it's time for urinating, with the help of warm sponges. Then rest. Already, each cub's personality has begun to show. The four black-furred Baribals are meek and mild. Youk 3 is so small that he is still unable to walk and mostly crawls. He is constantly being attacked by Youk 4, a bad-tempered female. Youk 5 is terrible. Jean-Jacques Annaud immediately nicknames him "Bad Nicky." Youk 8 is particularly cunning. She is the only one who leaves the nursery to go to the kitchen and observe the preparation of the baby bottles. Youk 9 is the most playful of the lot. Youk 10 and 11 love to be cuddled. Youk 12 is graciously distant. After one hour of play, the cubs need to rest. The crew lets them nap in their cages.

Wednesday, April 1

Jacques Allaire draws up a list of the animals that Jean-Philippe Varin will have to take along on location: two hundred birds, twenty pigeons, fifty quails, twenty mollusks, two hundred green frogs, five moor hens, five salamanders, twenty grasshoppers, five grass snakes, five hens, three ducks, ten moles, sixty seagulls. The director of the German part of the production must provide seventeen lizards, thirty ducks, five tortoises, fifteen crows, and twenty-five beehives.

Friday, April 3

Jean-Jacques Annaud meets Tchéky Karyo. For an hour the director narrates the story, insisting that it is the bears and not the hunters who are the stars of the film, that he is interested in the point of view of the hunted. All the while he is talking, Annaud observes the actor. He likes the actor's darting glance and deep blue eyes. But he does not promise anything yet. He is expecting cassettes from the United States and will consider other actors. Besides, he has not yet found anyone to play the other hunter, Bill. Tchéky heads home with the script under his arm. As he reads, he is breathing the clear mountain air, harkening to the rustling of the undergrowth, polishing his Winchester. He absolutely must have this role.

Monday, April 6

Jean-Jacques and Xavier watch video-castings taped in London and Los Angeles. They're worthless. Dissatisfied, the director calls London, once again explains his requirements, and orders a new casting call. He then meets with André Lacombe, to whom he'd like to give the role of Joseph, the man with the dogs.

Over sixty, with craggy cheeks, sunken eyes, and a salt-and-pepper beard, André Lacombe is a man who talks a lot and is not very savvy. To his potential director he makes some rather strange comments about *The Name of the Rose*, maintaining that he would have filmed certain scenes differently. Jean-Jacques lets him talk: the actor has a handsome face, and the character speaks only twice throughout the whole film.

André Lacombe is given the role of Joseph, who is in charge of the hunting dogs.

Tuesday, April 7

Not far from Paris, Jean-Jacques and Xavier spend the afternoon observing the training of the dog pack. When they arrive, six impressive Doberman pinschers are sitting in a boat in a pond that borders the house. André Noel then gathers the pack on the grass. With open mouths foaming and scarlet tongues, they form a threatening but beautiful group. They demonstrate an

Jean-Jacques gets to know his star better.

attack. One of the assistant trainers, wearing a sling covered by a bearskin, excites the dogs, which lunge at him one after the other, tearing at the fur with unbelievable force. Jean-Jacques is in heaven! On his way home, he makes a sudden turn and heads toward the local police station in order to deposit his driver's license, which has been suspended for a week for speeding two years before. The policemen, who know him well, are apologetic. As one of them says, "There are certain cases in which it is better to look the other way."

Friday, April 10

Jean-Jacques and Xavier meet Toni Ludi in the Dolomites. Equipped with snowshoes or sitting astride snowmobiles, they travel for miles along the mountains. The closest summit is six thousand feet high, the tallest eight thousand. The local mountain folk assure them that the snow will melt in time. Jean-Jacques realizes that physical stamina will play a major role during filming. Xavier's teeth are already chattering. But then, he is not properly dressed for the occasion. Jean-Jacques, however, is wearing real mountaineer's clothes: gaiters, thick wool socks, a triple-lined down parka, mittens. As always, he has left nothing to chance.

Satisfied, Jean-Jacques congratulates Ludi on locating the site.

In France, Jacques Allaire and the veterinarians are in the Sologne. The bear cubs are in perfect health and are brimming over with vitality. They climb on ladders, frisk about in the garden, and make a rumpus. One of them escapes the supervision of the nurses and plunges into the brambles. Just like a child, he cries loudly and rushes into his nurse's arms for comfort. Youk 4, always unbearable, rummages everywhere, attacks Jean-Philippe Varin's dog, and nibbles at the legs of Julie, the tamed deer of the house.

Sometimes punishment is meted out in the form of spankings, but then that turns into play. A spanking on the rump sends the cubs rolling, which, for them, is excellent exercise. In short, the future actors are irresistible.

Tuesday, April 14

Jean-Jacques and Xavier leave northern Italy for Hannover to meet the German trainer Dieter Kraml. The latter has purchased two brown cubs and will bring them on location, along with the twins. Xavier has asked him to train the two cubs with the female twins, in case anything goes wrong with Alfons Spindler's mother bear. But Kraml has not done anything yet. Jean-Jacques yells, and realizes that he may have to face more trouble down the road with this unpredictable, whimsical, and obstinate trainer.

Thursday, April 16

Jean-Jacques and Xavier depart for London.

On Air France Flight 808, departing at 8:30 A.M., the stewardesses smile at the familiar passengers.

At Jim Henson's studio, Ailsa Berk is rehearsing. She is concealed behind a foamy mold covered with brown cloth, her head hidden beneath a rigid helmet. She straightens herself up, stoops gracefully, sits down, seizes objects, pretends to eat, somersaults, and waves her hindquarters. Jean-Jacques is enjoying himself and would give anything to wear that outfit for a few minutes. Ray Scott presents the film director with a fake bear tongue. It is made up of fifteen segments, each about one centimeter wide, and is driven by four wires activated by two animatronics specialists. The tongue stretches, bends, and curves vigorously. The director congratulates the puppeteers on their talent.

In the afternoon, in a school that has been rented during the summer vacation, Jean-Jacques calls a meeting with the six mimes and for an hour and a half performs his favorite show. He starts from the very beginning of the storyboards and acts out every role, addressing himself to each mime in turn. Inexhaustible, he exhales, grinds his teeth, creases his nose, squats, lies down, simulates attack. He mimes Youk shaking before the big, lonely bear, or Kaar exhausted after sex, or Iskwao insatiably lusty, or Youk's mother, who is tender and warm. He becomes as sly as a fighting bear, as feline as the puma, and as disparaging as Kaar is of the hunters.

Saturday, April 18

In his dressing room at the mill, Jean-Jacques Annaud carefully prepares his trunks. From labeled drawers he removes articles of clothing that make up his impressive wardrobe: English sweaters, Hollywood socks, Canadian shoes, Italian jackets, French shirts, Australian raincoats. He has always been dapper. On his fourth birthday, when he had to cut his long blond curls, he made such a scene that a compromise had to be reached to calm the boy: as soon as the curls fell, a charming powder puff was placed on his head. As he fastens three trunks and two suitcases, the filmmaker remembers an amusing anecdote. Ever since playing in *Black and White in Color*, Jean Carmet, one of the actors, always provides the same answer to journalists who ask him about the film director. "He is a very clean, very well groomed, very elegant filmmaker."

Tuesday, April 21

Jean-Jacques leaves for New York. When he arrives at the Hotel Pierre, a stack of videocassettes awaits him at the reception desk. Sensing that they might contain the future Tom or Bill, the film director does not even bother to unpack. He turns on the VCR, takes out a sheet of paper, places it on his knees, and begins to jot down notes: "Bald; lacks violence." "No." "His eyes are too kind." "An interesting birthmark on his forehead." "Neither young nor old; uninteresting." "Horrible." "Fat alcoholic." "An idiot." "Huge; cross-eyed." "Drugged up." "A handsome look." "A nuthead immersed in thought." "Unbelievable teeth for a Western." "Handsome lad, but stupid." "Handsome face, too handsome." "A simpering pink fatso." "Not rustic enough." "Still another who loves his wife and kids." Amidst these gracious comments, only one name holds his attention: Jack Wallace. He is in his fifties and has a wonderful face that has aged well. Jean-Jacques arranges to meet him the following day.

Wednesday, April 22

In his apartment, Jack Wallace is getting ready to meet a French film director. Why has this director chosen him from among hundreds of others? He has been crisscrossing the United States for many years, putting on plays but making hardly any screen appearances. An hour later, sitting in the filmmaker's hotel suite, both feel as though they've known each other for many years. They hardly talk about *The Bear* at all. They talk about nature, about the recent death of Wallace's father, about *Quest for Fire* and *The Name of the Rose*, which the actor has seen and loved. With his lake-blue eyes and wrinkle-streaked face, which bespeaks generosity, Jean-Jacques thinks he'll make a splendid Bill. Cautious to the last, he puts off giving him an answer. He has yet to see what casting in Los Angeles and London may bring.

Thursday, April 23

From New York, Jean-Jacques flies to Los Angeles, where he auditions several actors but books none, then leaves for London. There he sees a dozen more actors, but all are disappointing.

Monday, April 27

Claude Berri leaves for London, where he meets Jean-Jacques Annaud at the special-effects studio. It is the first time that the producer comes to see the animatronics. The film director asks three of the puppeteers to activate Youk's and Kaar's heads. On demand, eyes shrink, gape wide open, nostrils quiver, ears move. Claude Berri cannot believe his eyes. Around twelve o'clock, Ailsa Berk arrives at the studio. She puts on the skin of Youk's mother and bear feet, which are nothing more than laced sneakers covered with foam. Claude Berri is worried and turns to Jean-Jacques: "Her shoelaces will show onscreen."

Delighted to see his producer spending the day in Disneyland, Jean-Jacques reassures him: the fur has not been glued on yet. Berri leaves the studio, happy with the visit but still worried about the schedule. Annaud must have ten scenes a day if he is to stay within the scheduled nineteen weeks, a frenetic pace indeed. But the filmmaker seems very relaxed. It is his last visit to London. He has an appointment on the film set. Very little time remains. The British team is working seventy-hour weeks so that everything will be ready on time.

Tuesday, April 28

From Heathrow airport, Jean-Jacques flies to Innsbruck, where Xavier Castano, Philippe Rousselot, and Toni Ludi await him. In the space of three eight-hour days, they will survey the Austrian mountains and define the film set for each scene. Every day is filled with hard work. Xavier is nicknamed "Cement Thighs," Jean-Jacques "Steel Thighs." The problem is that they are treading over areas that are still covered with snow. What is hidden underneath? This is a real puzzle for Toni and Philippe, especially since the director has decided to film certain scenes from the point of view of the bear cub, which means that the cameras will be placed at ground level. But what precisely does the ground consist of? Is it made of rocks, meadow, roots, or flowers?

Friday, May 1

The explorers cross the Italian border and stop close to Cortina d'Ampezzo, at San Vigilio, in the Dolomites. There is still a lot of snow, and it is firm and thick. Xavier has snow-blowers clear twelve miles of the route leading up to the location.

Monday, May 4

At San Vigilio, the first assistant adjusts his work schedule, keeping in mind the latest exploration of the sites. On which set will they begin filming, in Austria or in Italy? He opts for the Dolomites, where, according to the weather forecast, it is anticipated that the snow will thaw sooner than in the Tyrol.

But that night it snows three feet. For the first time, Jean-Jacques is worried. He calls Pierre Grunstein in Paris. The associate producer does not sound very pleased either. The mimes in London are on strike. Money transfers to the London banks have been so slow that the actors have not been paid yet. To make matters worse, they are supposed to begin training on location in forty-eight hours: no money, no trip. Everyone is in a bad mood.

Tuesday, May 5

Things could not be worse. Pierre receives a telephone call from Doug Seus, who is furious. The trainer has received the tickets for himself, his wife, his son-in-law, and Bart. But Bart's return ticket is missing. Seething with rage, the trainer decides that Bart will not leave Utah without a round-trip ticket. Pierre Grunstein tries to conceal his anxiety and to calm everyone involved. Only two men are happy at this time. Tchéky Karyo has just been told officially that he will play Tom. Upon hearing the news, the actor immediately leaves his apartment for his country home, where he intends to familiarize himself with his role. In New York, Jack Wallace's agent informs the actor that he has been given the role of Bill. He is thrilled to be working for Jean-Jacques Annaud, but the idea of filming in Europe does not excite him: planes make him airsick.

Thursday, May 7

While Tchéky Karyo rides horses, breaks walls, plants trees, wanders all over the mountains, carts away stones, and perfects his English, Xavier,

Doc, in his cage, waits on the film set on Cinque Terre in northern Italy.

Philippe, and Jean-Jacques watch the snow fall on the Dolomites. At the hotel in San Vigilio, the bellboy knocks at Annaud's door. He hands him a telegram, the contents of which are crushing. The authorizations that the authorities in Rome had given him to film on his chosen sites have been summarily revoked. Local peasants, supported by their mayor, have signed a petition against the project. The village, in fact, is divided in two factions: on one side the hotels, on the other the peasants and the mayor. Three years ago, the mayor had wanted to dig a sand pit. The peasants supported the project; the hotel managers opposed it. Today, the hotels would love to welcome two hundred people during their slow season. By refusing them permission to film, the mayor is having his revenge. Jean-Jacques is shattered. What is to be done? Try to persuade the mayor and the peasants? After much hesitation, he decides to scout for a new location—eleven days before filming is scheduled to start.

Mark Wiener, Doc, and Grizz have left their home and are headed for Los Angeles. He is scheduled to take off for Frankfurt at 3:30 P.M. on Lufthansa Flight 441. Settled in the two cages especially built for them, the bears fly over the Atlantic and prepare to discover Europe.

Friday, May 8

Customs officials watch some strange tourists disembark at the Frankfurt airport. It is now 11:20 A.M. and the customs offices close at noon. The clerks do not want to know anything. It is impossible to let two bears through in half an hour on the day before the weekend. Mark Wiener is furious. Europe is an impossible continent. He calls up the producer, insults the customs officials. Meanwhile, the two fifteen-hundred-pound monsters have a certain effect on the customs officials and are finally allowed to pass. Doc and Grizz leave the airport and head to the north of the city, to spend the night in an animal park, the Lug Animal Station.

Ninety-three miles away from San Vigilio, Jean-Jacques, Xavier, Philippe, and Toni scout a new location near Misurina, at an altitude of eight thousand feet. The depth of the snow is such that it is impossible to start filming the scene with Youk and his mother. Jean-Jacques decides to begin with the torrent and undergrowth scene, at an altitude of six thousand feet, where the snow is beginning to melt. Xavier telephones the British team, which is dumbstruck. This change in their work schedule forces them to rush in order to finish the animatronic model of Kaar's head, which is necessary for the scene in the undergrowth. Meanwhile, the mimes have received their paychecks. They start rehearsing again, but how will they make up for the delay?

Saturday, May 9

Doc's and Grizz's trailers cross the Italian border and arrive in Misurina at night. Pierre Grunstein and Claude Berri are already on location to give moral support.

In Clermont-Ferrand, Madame Sauvadet leaves the zoo, having "packed" Bad Nicky, and heads for Jean-Philippe Varin's home in Sainte-Montaine.

Monday, May 11

Doug Seus is in a better mood. Bart's return ticket has arrived this morning. In Sainte-Montaine, a huge truck, two cars, and a station wagon are set to leave. Crammed together are eight bear cubs in their cages, hundreds of animals, millions of insects, the five nursemaids, an entomologist, and Varin. The procession is joined by Madame Sauvadet and François Hugues.

They are all en route to northern Italy. This evening, the caravan will cross the border at Kiel, in Germany. Tomorrow evening it will arrive in Misurina.

Tuesday, May 12

From Heber City, Doug Seus's trailer, carrying Bart and all of his two thousand pounds, sets out for Los Angeles. Lufthansa Flight 441, destination Frankfurt, departs at 3:30 P.M.

Varin and his caravan cross the Austrian border at Innsbruck and proceed to Bolzano, in northern Italy. They arrive at Misurina in the evening and are welcomed by Maryvonne Leclerc-Cassan.

Wednesday, May 13

The trainers settle the bears down near the village of Misurina. Four months old now, the Baribals begin to display their distinctive features. With their fur now blacker, ears more pointed, and noses longer, they are less charming than the brown bear cubs. Each has a surname and an appointed "mother." Nathalie, who has a weakness for the Baribals, cares for Youk 1; Youk 2; Youk 6, called "Blackcurrant"; and Youk 7, called "Casserole Dish." Maguy cares for Youk 3, called "Gogol"; and Youk 9, called "Panda." Madame Sauvadet is raising Bad Nicky with great difficulty.

Noël Vandendries and his daughter care for Youk 8, called "Kiwi"; Youk 10, called "Cadix"; and Youk 11, called "Cadence." And Marie-France watches over the intrepid Youk 4, called "Zazou"; and Youk 12, so distant, so remote, that no one is interested in her, even though someone must take care of her.

In the evening, the English crew arrives and requisitions two entire floors of the Hotel Lavaredo.

Friday, May 15

Jean-Jacques visits Doug Seus and explains the details of the scene to be filmed on the first day. Doug had been told he would have three weeks to train his Kodiak on the set. Because of the scheduling changes due to the snow, the director informs the trainer that they have been forced to start shooting with the torrent sequence. Doug feels Bart is not yet ready, so Jean-Jacques turns to his understudy, Doc.

Sunday, May 17

In Misurina, the traffic is intense. English, French, Italians, Germans, Austrians, Swiss, Americans have invaded the hotels: all told, 180 persons. That evening, in the nightclub of the Hotel Lavaredo, the film director has a drink and introduces himself to each group of technicians. Then, with microphone, Xavier reads the set instructions, which are translated into four languages:

Doc is ready to be filmed. Hot wires separate him from the camera, located less than six feet away.

"On all film sets, protective electric wires will be installed. They are invisible

and dangerous. It is forbidden to eat on the set near the animals. When the animals are out of their cages, it is forbidden to run or to make unnecessary movements. Only the necessary personnel will be allowed on the set. As soon as the director shouts 'Action,' no one may move until the bears are returned to their cages after filming. The bear cubs, who seem very cute, are extremely dangerous. Only the nursemaids are allowed to touch them. Veterinary examinations and inspections by the associations for the protection of animals and nature will take place every week."

Next it is Pierre Grunstein's turn: "All of us together, for a period of five months, under very strenuous conditions, are going to share an experience that we hope will be unique. Thank you for working with us."

Jean-Jacques concludes: "Good night. See you tomorrow."

Filming
THE
BEAR

Monday, May 18, 1987: six o'clock in the morning. A frozen dawn is rising over Misurina. The village, made up of no more than seven hotels and eight restaurants on a road leading to Cortina d'Ampezzo, twelve miles away, has something phantasmagoric about it: two rows of buildings in the middle of nowhere. The mountains begin in back of each building. Out of season, when the tourists have left, Misurina ceases to exist.

On this morning a violent, gusty wind blows through eddies of lashing rain. Shivering outlines rush out of four hotels, which have been specially opened at the request of *The Bear*'s producers, and just as quickly disappear inside a minibus whose engine is already running. In the meantime, several hundred miles away, the Cannes Film Festival is preparing to honor Federico Fellini's latest film, *Intervista*, with a spectacular ovation. Jean-Jacques Annaud, at the age of forty-three, is about to start his fifth full-length film in a blizzard.

Outside the city, the road runs along a pleasant lake similar to dozens that dot the Dolomites. In the middle of this frozen expanse, ice forms a stalagmite that juts skyward as a vision in some imaginary tale. In the caravan of thirty minibuses, no one enjoys this unusual spectacle. Each technician is thinking the same thought: lousy weather. It is the first day of a shoot that is to take at least four months, and it has already started poorly.

Hidden behind the rock, Jean-Philippe Varin is ready to help out if there is any trouble with the cub.

May 18, 1987: the first day of shooting. Douce is "discovered"—she outshines the other cubs and Annaud decides to make her the lead star.

Half an hour later, at an altitude of six thousand feet, the temperature has fallen a few more degrees by the time the cars reach their destination, the Fanes River. The crew plunges into the underbrush and discovers a sixty-five-foot-wide torrent. Here is the first set of the first scene to be filmed.

The storyboards indicate: *Kaar crosses a torrent; Youk hestitates and then dashes in.* The sentence describes a situation the outcome of which no one, not even the director, knows precisely. Of course, Jean-Jacques has carefully imagined, conceived, and prepared each of the seventeen hundred sketches that make up the storyboards. He knows them all by heart and can roll his film in his mind with photographic precision. Filming for him is usually nothing more than a series of "taping sessions." All the same, anything can happen. For the first time in his career, he is more or less at the mercy of his unpredictable actors. Will Kaar cross the torrent? And after how many takes? *Youk hesitates.* How can a cub convey this?

This morning, even the most seasoned technicians are asking themselves what unanticipated difficulties will arise. The first day of filming is always a leap into the unknown. This time everyone's curiosity is even more intense than usual. The filmmaker is using the only reasonable option: given his inability to predict exactly how the animals will behave during filming, by focusing three cameras on them he stands a better chance of capturing a gaze, a movement, a gesture.

Technicians venture out into the icy water to set up the first camera, where Jean-Jacques and the Italian cameraman Michele Picciaredda are standing. On another bank, Philippe Rousselot is put in charge of the second camera, in addition to his function as director of photography. With the third camera on the opposite bank are Arnaud du Boisberranger and Xavier Castano, whom Jean-Jacques has made director of the second crew, in addition to his role as first assistant. Jean-Jacques has given each cameraman a specific responsibility. Michele's first task is to ascertain the infallibility of the main camera, the "master." Second, he is to provide a precise description of the action he has filmed. Philippe's filming will be broader, without very complicated shots, so that he can concentrate on lighting. Arnaud's responsibility is originality, risk, inventiveness.

Twelve cages containing the film's stars appear on the set. In the face of these furry balls the crew rediscovers the curiosity of their own childhood. The proportions of the cubs, their feet, their ears, their chubby tummies, and their faces, at once funny, gracious, brazen, and shy, fascinate even the most blasé.

Cared for by their affectionate nursemaids, the cubs are given a small white mark on each shoulder so they resemble each other and then are dropped into the torrent. Wearing wet suits, the trainers observe the results of months of training from behind the rocks. Surprised at being thrust into the water so soon, the cubs grab the first rock or swim to the opposite bank. Those who dislike the water are filmed only once. Bad Nicky is absolutely fiendish. He stamps his feet with rage like a spoiled brat and, with his claws, tears open Madame Sauvadet's cheek. Pierre Grunstein immediately takes her to the hospital. Gogol, the smallest of the bunch, is so light that the undertow carries him away before he is able to react. Others behave like model students. But in the space of a few hours, Jean-Jacques Annaud discovers the one cub who will become his main star: Youk 12, called "Douce." She has a delightful face and is the only one to adapt to the situation with grace and nonchalance. Indifferent to the tumult of the torrent, insensitive to the cold, she approaches the crew with disarming innocence. The originality of her behavior, the expressions on her face, her openness impress, seduce, and touch the director. As though by magic, she performs each sketch of the storyboards. The nursemaids are dumbfounded. Independent from birth, Douce avoided her mother's caresses. The other cubs will be Douce's stand-ins. Jean-Jacques already plans to get rid of Bad Nicky and the four Baribals, all of whom look too different to blend with the others.

Toward afternoon, the big, solitary bear, whom nobody has yet seen, must make his first appearance on the set. Crouching down in his cage, Doc waits for the technicians to prepare the set. Electric wires, like those used to pen in grazing cows, are stretched along stakes planted every thirty feet and spray-painted to blend into the background. These live wires define the animal's territory. He has been trained to understand that he is forbidden to cross this barrier, which separates him from the cameras. The second assistant director is ready to activate the current at the command of the director should the animal stray even the slightest bit.

"Silence. Let no one move. Doc is coming out of his cage," says Xavier. Conversation stops, everyone's gaze is drawn toward the colossal beast. Scared and petrified, the crew watches this gigantic mass approach Mark Wiener and step slowly into the water. Almost blind, as all bears are, Doc is guided by the words "Good boy, good boy," which the torrent echoes, and by the odor of raw fish and sweets, which his trainer throws him from the riverbank. The bear seems to enjoy the situation. He advances into the water calmly and,

Before a scene, the trainer
Mark Wiener exhorts his bear:
"Listen, Doc, when you're
done you're going to get a
nice chicken."

Doc's first appearance in the
torrent as he looms toward the
film crew.

nearing a rock, delicately places his paws on it. A whitish fog rises, and the rock disappears. It was made of stucco. The technicians realize that the slightest unplanned gesture can reduce them to pulp.

Between takes, Doc stuffs himself. One of the fundamentals of training is to deprive the animal of food for a few hours before he must perform and of rewarding him generously after he performs. By the end of the day, Doc will have consumed twenty-six pounds of food: six chickens, four barrels of marshmallows, ten trout, and thirty bottles of apple juice.

6:00 P.M.: the engines are turned off. Soaked and numb with cold, the crew returns to Misurina. Many begin to dread the four months to come. At the same time they are very excited. Maybe it's like the feeling of covering a news story. Whenever a bear moved during the takes, Jean-Jacques Annaud would film it—even if the trainers, the electric fence, chicken legs, sweets, or fish tails were shot.

The following day, Pierre Grunstein advises Madame Sauvadet to return to France to complete the education of her "little brat." Meanwhile, at 6:00, the crew takes the Fanes River road and makes its way into the damp underbrush that borders the torrent. In a corner of the set, the prop people run from tree to tree carrying a giant atomizer filled with strawberry syrup. Michele's and Philippe's cameras focus on a tree trunk, while, strapped to a branch, from a high-angle perspective, Arnaud du Boisberranger's camera awaits the colossus. Scene: *Kaar, enjoying rubbing his back against a tree trunk, is hit by a pine cone.*

"Careful. Mark Wiener is releasing the bear." Tempted by the sweetish smell, Doc gets closer, inspects the trees, and flattens his back against one of them. Amazed, the technicians watch him perform: the bear has decided to rub himself against the same trunk the director wanted him to rub against. Everyone has forgotten that this exercise is one of a bear's favorite sports. Hidden away among the branches, Arnaud, all the while filming, throws a pine cone. He misses. He tries again, misses again. On his fourth attempt, he hits Doc right in the middle of his snout. Jean-Jacques smiles, delighted. The scene matches the sketch on the storyboards. But the actor is much less delighted. From the top of his nine-foot height, the bear catches sight of the guilty party. Vindictively, Doc attacks the trunk, which begins to sway violently. Arnaud fears that his career will end suddenly, somewhere in the Dolomites. But the trainer reacts immediately. Swinging a plump chicken, he diverts the actor's attention and saves an excellent cameraman. On the set,

"Good boy, good boy," the trainers tirelessly repeat after each take.

the tension has mounted. And yet, the crew feels attracted by this fascinating danger, which promises powerful emotions.

To calm the general anxiety, Jean-Jacques films the scene in which Kaar sniffs out and finds the mushrooms. Crawling on the ground, the director places them one after the other, looks through his viewfinder, flattens himself on the ground, readjusts them, and starts filming. Doc, whose bad mood has been dispelled, is in top form. Amusing, inventive, he outperforms the storyboards and, moreover, enjoys himself. The mushrooms may look real, but they are made of almond paste.

The third day brings no improvement in the weather. Walking slowly, twenty-five Englishmen arrive on the set. They are towing a trailer in which, like the decapitated head of a pagan statue, lies Kaar's animatronic head. For the special-effects team this moment is crucial, because it concretizes months of relentless work, as well as cruel, because in London this latex head seemed beautiful and here, covered with fur, it looks dull next to its living model. The English team, which worked from photographs sent by the bear's trainer, realizes immediately how disappointing its product is. Sadly the puppeteers

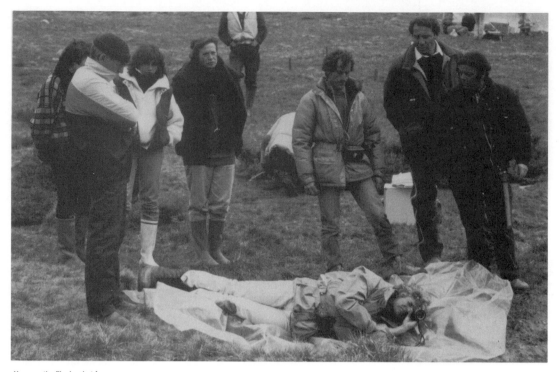

place the head on the set, hook up the wires, and rehearse the movements. The installation takes four hours.

Meanwhile, Jean-Jacques films close-ups of the real bear. Because he is filmed at various speeds, his reactions are stunningly different. When the British team is ready, Jean-Jacques realizes that the animatronic head offers a limited spectrum of expressions. Squatting near their remote controls, ten puppeteers activate the animatronic wires, and each one, as in a silent film, reproduces on his face the very movements he commands. Despite the puppeteers' talent, the results are mediocre. Wrap-up time comes. Jean-Jacques leaves the set perturbed. What can be done? If the fake bears are disappointing, what solutions are available for the filming of scenes that cannot be staged with real bears? All he can do is hope that the real bears will give of their very best and convince the trainers to go beyond the limits they agreed upon. He knows that this film provides them with a unique opportunity to prove their expertise. Till now, their bears have acted for a few minutes in long films or seconds in commercials. In his film, however, the bears will be onscreen for an hour and thirty minutes.

At the end of the week, Jean-Jacques Annaud feels much more confident: the bears and cubs have shown such grace, charm, and strength that their natural qualities will provide invaluable, unexpected assets. There is only one piece of bad news: when the director and his first assistant reached eight thousand feet, near Fiera di Primiero, fifty miles from Misurina, to scout the scenery for the opening sequence of the film—the scene with the cub and his mother—seven feet of snow concealed everything. The wind blew so hard that the two men were unable to stand. Worried, they returned to the village and shut themselves up in their hotel. The director had wanted to film the story chronologically, but it is still impossible to shoot the opening sequence.

Two hours later, the director decides to alter his work plan. The opening scene is shifted around, and the crew, to its dismay, finds out that it must relocate. Pierre Grunstein has been unable to obtain authorization from the local government to have the hotels stay open during the slow season.

An enormous amount of film, 42,650 feet, has already been shot. But the director knows things will improve in the weeks to come. These first few days were crucial. Every body movement, every facial expression seemed so precious that it was vital to capture it.

Departure: 7:00 A.M.; destination: Fiera di Primiero. During the day, the trucks unload all the material at the location, twenty miles from the hotel, at Lago di Calaita. Varin and the cubs' nursemaids settle in the village of Prado, next to the set. In the public garden, the zoological advisor hoists a large tent. Under the covering, he places large cages for the cubs and builds shelves where glass cases containing toads, frogs, lizards, mollusks, and squirrels are placed. Outside, grasshoppers, pigeons, and doves inspect the surroundings. The butterflies that the entomologists hunted with love and a sense of delicacy days before are preserved in an isothermic box in a semi-frozen state. This system allows them to wake up gently while the cameras are preparing to roll and to start flying only after they have been warmed by the surrounding air.

Immediately aware of the presence of this strange crew, the entire village arrives to take stock of what will later make them proud.

Sixteen hundred feet farther up, the German trainers Dieter Kraml and Alfons Spindler finish building cages: one for each of the twins, both of whom will play Youk's mother; the third for a tame mother bear who will play the mother, and her two cubs, who will play Youk; and finally, the fourth, for the cubs that Dieter Kraml raised to serve as stand-ins for Douce. Late in the afternoon, Kraml arrives in the village square with the twins on a leash. Seeing the public crowding toward him, he sits on a bench with a bear on each side, providing an improvised, free circus show.

That night Jean-Jacques receives a call from the producer, Claude Berri: "I've just seen the rushes of the torrent scene. I'm really thrilled. The power of the big bear, the spontaneity of the small one, the photography, it's all really fantastic. But the marks on the cub's shoulders are too visible, much too white. You must try to blur them a bit."

Puzzled, the film director hangs up and calls the editor, Noëlle Boisson, who tells him: "Listen. I've been an editor for fifteen years, and I know when something exceptionally rare is taking place onscreen. In the space of a few seconds, Douce moved me. I felt like taking her in my arms. She has the charisma of a real star. She'll dominate the screen."

"And what about the white marks?"

"Maybe we're going to have to tone them down somewhat. You see them less and less as you move from one frame to the next."

"Signor Annaud, two more calls for you."

First, it's his agent. He is categorical: it's fantastic. But the white marks look artificial. Then it is Pierre Grunstein, who has gone to Paris especially to view a more polished showing. The director has nothing to worry about. Only a few seconds' worth of frames will need editing.

Annaud is nevertheless bothered. The difficulty arises from the fact that some of the cubs have natural white marks on their shoulders. The make-up artist, Hans Jurgen Schmelzle, can be be extremely resourceful with paintbrushes and spray cans, but touch-up jobs are very delicate. These problems are very annoying. The viewing of rushes in continuity is a thankless test that belongs to no one but the director, but he is the only one who has not seen anything yet. Exasperated that everyone else has seen the rushes before him, he goes upstairs to bed, grumbling to himself, "I envy them."

To reach the immense, windy plateau of Lago di Calaita, surrounded by rocky mountains, vehicles trundle along the bumpy road. Then, with their arms loaded with all sorts of equipment and materials, the technicians must cross the last two hundred yards on foot to reach the set. On the damp yellow plain, fake frogs jump about, propelled by the entomologist. The frog is the first animal Youk meets. Two cubs try the role in turn. In the background, the nursemaids comfort their wards with the tender words of mothers: "Come on, sweetheart, come on, don't be afraid."

Between takes, each nursemaid rushes toward her cub, rolls up her sleeves, and lets the cub suck on her arm. The cubs purr with pleasure, a strange, monotonous tone that sounds like that of a swarm of bees.

"Varin, release the real frogs. I'll use Douce."

Douce's behavior is very amusing. Whenever she is surprised, she leaps backward, finds her balance, jumps up with her four paws spread out, lands clumsily, and hurls herself about in a funny, acrobatic dance. Annaud is ecstatic. He lets the cameras roll until they are out of film. "Good. That's very good. Now let's film the scene in which Youk is nostalgic."

But Douce has a strong personality. It is difficult to get her to act sad.

"Maguy, can you calm her down?"

Dipping her hands into a can filled with oat flakes mixed with rice and carrots, the nursemaid feeds the cub. Douce is smeared up to her ears. Hans, the make-up artist, cleans her and turns her into a beauty while the cub is busy sucking on Maguy's arm. Marie-France, Douce's true adoptive mother, witnesses the scene. Frustrated, she exclaims: "Of course she sucks badly. She misses her mommy." The crew can't suppress their giggles.

Action! Douce comes out of a pond, climbs over a hillock, and sits down.

Now she is supposed to turn around, looking nostalgic, before Michele's camera. But she doesn't. Instead, she rolls out of the camera's frame and prances away. The second take is no better.

"Maguy, she is still too agitated. Put her to sleep, if you can." An hour goes by. Silently the crew watches the nursemaid, who, with her sweet caresses, manages to put the cub to sleep.

Action! Douce is sleeping. At the sound of the director's whistle, she opens an eye, lifts her head, yawns, and falls asleep again. Jean-Jacques congratulates Maguy. Marie-France makes a face. But where is Philippe Rousselot? For hours, with both feet in a pond, he has been struggling with a case built by the technical team to hold the underwater camera. The plan is to film the scene from the vantage point of the frog. Water leaks into the case. Philippe patches it up. But he is a poet of lighting, not a mechanic. Exhausted, he groans.

The cold, uninterrupted rain is so violent that the technicians, packed together like sardines, take shelter under whatever they happen to find. There's nothing doing. The sky won't clear up.

"Jean-Jacques, the rushes have arrived. They're waiting for you at the movie theater in Fiera."

It's a catastrophe. The projectionist is dead drunk and has not touched his projector in years. It is rusted, and the lens seems to have been filed with sandpaper.

The first pictures are blurry and out of focus. And then the film catches on fire. Rousselot is discouraged. The director calls a halt and returns to his hotel, where the videocassettes have just been delivered. A VCR and television set have been placed in the hotel bar for just this purpose. In the evening, tourists and crew members sit and watch the soccer game. The VCR is not working. It takes an hour to repair it. Jean-Jacques waits, trying to suppress his anger. Finally it works. The only cassette that interests the director is the one filmed in the torrent. He wants to check on the white marks on the cubs. Bad luck. This cassette has been taped on a different system and cannot be viewed. Jean-Jacques does not even have the strength to grumble. He goes to dinner in a bad mood, which he conceals under a smile.

"God, remember *The Name of the Rose*," proclaims the director at 7:30 A.M. on the eleventh day of filming, pointing toward the sky. But the sky over the immense plateau of Lago di Calaita has no memory, and the icy rain continues to fall. Despite the mud, Jean-Jacques Annaud wears his tenth set of clothing since filming began, his third pair of insulated shoes with triple soles, and his fourth parka. Around his waist he buckles a belt on which are strapped five pouches, each containing things he would never want to be without: wind-resistant matches, an asbestos survival blanket, a mirror, an anti-mosquito hat, sun lotion, a thermometer, an altimeter, a trumpet, a whistle, a compass, a bonnet, mittens, a scarf, snow glasses, nose drops, throat lozenges, a magnifying glass, a twenty-function Swiss army knife. His fastidious habits are the subject of gentle ribbing on the part of the crew.

Jean-Jacques begins a scene that is very important because it leads into the first scene of the encounter between the big bear and the orphaned cub: *Wounded, Kaar, limps through mud holes. Youk approaches and licks his wound. A soothing shiver runs down Kaar's spine, and he lets the cub continue.* A mysterious pact will exist between the colossus and the orphan. It is this complicity between the two and the emotions that follow in its wake that the director wishes to convey to the audience.

The schedule allows five days to film these scenes. Eight will be needed, and they will seem to last forever.

It's 8:00 A.M. Doug Seus arrives on location with his wife, Lynne, his son-in-law, Clint, and the sixteen foot trailer. While Doug and Clint set up the hot wires around several acres, Lynne sets up the "groceries." In a row on the ground are innumerable crates of fruits and vegetables, fifty jars of jam, and crates of apple juice.

"Nobody move. Bart is coming out of his cage," shouts Xavier. Although Bart, who weighs 450 pounds more than Doc, is much more impressive, he is also more reassuring. He seems to be amazingly affectionate toward his trainer.

"Good boy, good boy, Bart. Sit. Stay!"

The relationship between the trainer and the bear is incredible. It had impressed Jean-Jacques and Pierre when they first visited Utah, in 1983. But now it rivets all 180 members of the crew. Bart hugs his master tightly against him, licks him, picks him up.

"Stop, Bart. Come here!"

A bear's colossal food supply for a single day during shooting.

94

To simulate the bear's wound, the make-up artist has made a sort of scab that looks like gored flesh covered with hair. While Clint feeds Bart sweets, Doug applies the fake wound on his left shoulder and sprays it with fake blood. Placidly, the bear lets his master do as he pleases. In fact, the trainer has been gluing a fake wound on the same spot every day for a whole year.

"Doug, I don't want to put pressure on your bear. Let him do what he wants. As long as he limps while walking, whatever he feels like doing is good for me too," says Jean-Jacques; then, nevertheless, he explains in detail what he wants.

He then beckons to Xavier: "Please imitate a bear." The first assistant director stoops and runs from mud hole to mud hole, mimicking the bear down to its very limp.

Two movable platforms, each fifteen feet by five feet, are placed on the ground for Philippe's and Arnaud du Boisberranger's cameras. Michele is to aim at the ground. Fake trees conceal the trainers.

12:00 P.M.: Bart is on the plain, 330 feet away from the cameras. Action! The bear approaches. "Give me a limp, give me a limp," pleads Doug.

Bart limps once, twice, three times, then stops. He downs ten apple juices, two chickens. He limps again. He eats again. He limps again. But it's not enough. Doug has spent two whole years teaching Bart to run on three paws and tuck the forth under his breast. And now, on the crucial day, he lets him down. In desperation, the trainer pours blueberry jelly into a pan with a very long handle. It has taken Doug three weeks to design this pan and one to manufacture it. Its purpose is to lure Bart while allowing the trainer to remain out of the frame. Forgetting to use the long handle, he holds the pan so close to Bart that he appears in the shot as well. It is both comic and pathetic. And yet this bear, who limps for the benefit of a film scene and not just for a circus number, has earned everyone's admiration.

After lunch, it's the same scene, but this time in close-up: first take, second take, twentieth take. Bart has eaten so much that he is bloated. He wants only one thing: to take a nap. But the realities of filmmaking do not allow for this. Doug yells: "No, don't sit. Back. Give me a limp."

Unruffled, the director explains the movements once again. Doug doesn't know where to turn. He blends salmon, carrots, milk, marshmallows, chicken, and apples in the pan. Bart continues to gorge himself, but refuses to work. Doug feels very embarrassed. He gets hold of a long whip, which the bear stuffs into his mouth while the trainer pulls from the other end. The crew

Bart allows a fake wound to be applied to his left shoulder and then it is sprayed with fake blood. Pictured here, from left to right: Doug Seus, his wife, Lynne, and son-in-law Clint Youngreen.

In one of the scenes, Kaar is supposed to limp, and for two years Bart has been trained to imitate this.

watches this unusual fight between two gladiators, from which Doug emerges victorious.

This has been a difficult day for the director, typifying one of the major obstacles to filming. If the bears are fit, each take may last thirty minutes. If they feel lazy, out of sorts, or frivolous, each take may require several days. What is needed is not just a lot of confidence but inexhaustible patience.

This is exactly what Claude Berri believes when he shows up on the following day. Berri, who considers himself "the best director among producers, and the best producer among directors," obviously hates watching others filming. It bores him to death, especially this film, which requires a degree of patience and tenacity he can never have.

"At best, I might have made a short film," he confides to the director, "but a full-length feature film, never."

Then he turns around, feeling a cub brushing against him. "Ah! Here is my film star." Holding Douce in his arms, he adds, "To think that on her shoulders rides one and a half million dollars."

"Everyone at their station," shouts Jean-Jacques Annaud.

Everything is set up as on the previous day. Bart, who seems to have

Three cameras simultaneously record Doc as he soothes himself in the mud hole.

remembered the script from the night before, makes for the first mud hole, proceeds to the next, and, reclining on the correct side, soothes his wound in the third, in a sequence shot.

"He is the Marlon Brando of bears," exclaims a highly impressed Berri.

That evening, because the Hotel Iris in Fiera di Primiero is hosting a convention on the fourth floor, the crew has had to relocate. They head for San Martino, eight miles away. It is a small, isolated, dull village. Two hotels have opened to receive the crew. At the Savoia, the morale is low. The rooms are small. There are no bathtubs, only showers. And Xavier is there as the the bearer of bad tidings. The technicians rush to his room to find out that they are to spend five weeks there.

As soon as Jean-Jacques has unpacked his three trunks and two suitcases, he crosses the village's only street and enters the Belvedere Residence, where the English team has taken over the Ping-Pong room to create a special-effects area. They are in the process of finishing Kaar's skin for the mime who is to use it the next day. The director asks the mime Michael Blair to put on the fur. In order to test its believability, they take a stroll around the town. A motorcyclist who happens to be speeding by is so surprised at seeing this huge mass crossing the street in front of him that he nearly has a fatal crash.

The British team hardly sleeps that night. At 7:00 A.M. they appear on the set at Lago di Calaita. It takes three hours for an eight-person team to help Michael Blair put on the suit. Baldwyn, the French mime, watches his understudy gradually disappear under the fur and feels disappointed that he will not be playing Kaar's role today. His suit is still being manufactured; apparently the special-effects people have opted to help one of their nationals.

As soon as he arrives, Jean-Jacques asks the mimes to stand next to Bart's cage so that their make-up can be adjusted. Seeing the real bear, the British team realizes once again the difficulty of the situation. The difference is striking. The texture of the synthetic fur lacks life, lacks that special silky sheen. But what can be done? Despite the drawbacks of the fake fur, the British crew heeds Doug Seus's advice not to use real fur, for the bears might mistake the mimes for real bears, and a fight would be unavoidable. At any rate, since the scene in question is impossible to produce with two real bears, filming cannot begin before 11:00 A.M.

The mime coordinator, Ailsa Berk (five feet tall), accompanies the artificial bear (nine feet) to the mud hole. The disproportion in size is both touching and slightly ridiculous.

The director tells Michael Blair to lie down in the mud hole and asks whether it feels comfortable. A grunting negative is all the answer he gets. The director swears never to ask him the same question. An English doctor stands next to the mime with an oxygen bottle. The make-up artist glues a brand-new wound to the mime's left shoulder and then pours onto it a red liquid blended with caramel. Douce should find it delicious. From his forty-foot-high gantry, Jean-Jacques directs the operations with his walkie-talkie.

Action! The director indicates to the mime the movements he must perform in relation to those of the bear.

Ignoring the camera, and oblivious to what is happening on the set, Douce gallops onto the plain. Jean-Jacques calls to the cub's nursemaid: "Marie-France, lie down in the mud next to the mime, and then beckon to your bear." The nursemaid stoops down as low as possible. "Lower; you're still in the frame," shouts Jean-Jacques. Flattened next to the fake bear skin, Marie-France tries to hide herself even more. "Lower, lower," shouts Jean-Jacques. Frozen, covered with mud, the nursemaid squashes down until she blends in with the mud. "Perfect," observes the director. "Now, don't move." A

Douce

99

plaintive but scarcely audible groan emerges from Marie-France's mouth: "Come, my sweetheart, please come quickly."

But Douce does not care. Varin, hiding behind a tree, tries calling the cub. The cub does not know which of the two to heed. Jean-Jacques feels that the day is drawing to a close. Unable to wait much longer, from the top of his gantry, through his walkie-talkie, he repeats the nursemaid's words, "Come, sweetheart, my baby, my darling," in loud, stern, paternal tones. It's a miracle! "Sweetheart" lopes toward the mime, takes a liking to caramel, climbs over the bear fur, and finally licks, licks, licks. Cut!

It is 7:00 P.M. Ailsa rushes to Michael Blair and helps him out of his costume. Tired, flushed, and faint, the mime runs onto the plain, barefoot, wearing only his briefs. Reduced to his six-foot-eight-inch frame, he is silhouetted against the wind and the rain.

But this hellish scene is not yet finished; four more days are needed. The perpetually oppressive sky, the clouds hanging over the mountaintops, the poor

In the fog, Douce waits for the sun to break through so filming can resume.

100

visibility, the weather worse than ever, all lend an apolcalyptic aura to these days. Penned in by thick fog, which makes the fog machine seem altogether ridiculous, Philippe, Michele, and Arnaud nevertheless set up the cameras. Wrapped in a huge, ankle-length raincoat purchased in Sydney, the director treads frantically back and forth along the plain for four straight days. Although Jean-Jacques is ready to start filming the moment he steps out of his hotel, he will often find himself idle because of adverse weather conditions. So, in order to take his mind off things and boost morale, he takes a few shots of salamanders and insects. Dripping wet, Philippe deploys his artillery, setting up a staggering array of projectors. An uninformed visitor might think he has strayed into a film version of Napoleon's campaign in Russia. A more observant visitor would realize that they are filming toads who have lost their way in the fog.

Pierre Grunstein is worried. Repeating Claude Berri's magical sentence "It's not what a film costs that matters, but what it earns," the associate producer goes over his figures. The fact is, due to horrible weather conditions, expenses have been mounting by the day. To reduce costs, he decides to part with the English mime Michael Blair, thinking that one mime (Baldwyn) should be more than sufficient. He also sends one of the Youk nurses back to France with the four Baribal cubs, Youk 1, Youk 2, Blackcurrant, and Casserole Dish, whose features have grown increasingly different from those of the brown bears.

On the eighth day of this interminable sequence, the sky finally begin to clear. The special-effects people, set designers, assistants, cameramen, trainers, and director unleash a determined energy spurred by the hope of getting the job done as quickly as possible. At night, they sing and celebrate their patience and tenacity until dawn.

Back in the village of Imer, Doug Seus knows that this film represents the most important motion picture in Bart's career and can reflect well on his own reputation in addition. For days Doug has been thinking. In conversations with his wife and his son-in-law he has come up with a plan. This crazy plan contradicts the laws of nature, the tenets of specialists, and the intentions that both the film director and the associate producer have been nursing for five years. Determined to bring about his project, Doug visits Pierre Grunstein at the production department's office. "What about training a cub with Bart? Mimes and animatronics are nonsense."

Clearly, the trainer's proposition throws Grunstein off balance. The way Doug explains it, it sounds tempting. Besides, the bears and the cubs are irresistible, and the animatronics are the only persistent problem for Jean-Jacques Annaud. The English crew works night and day, the make-up artists keep trying to improve the color of the fur, and the sculptors are continually altering the forms for the skin. The animatronics could be sufficiently perfected, provided there is enough time. But the schedule is tight.

Pierre is undecided. Biological reality suggests that a bear of Bart's size would make a quick meal of any cub not directly related to it. On the other hand, Pierre not only is aware of the trainer's undisputed reputation, but has also seen him at work in Utah and, above all, remembers a cassette the trainer had sent him that impressed him very much. At the time when the production company was planning to shoot the film in the United States, Doug and Clint had started training Bart with a bear cub from a neighboring area. The results were stunning. Despite his two thousand pounds, Bart looked like a big fat teddy bear leading a peaceful, familiar existence under the absolute authority of his trainer.

The veterinarians, François Hugues and Maryvonne Leclerc-Cassan, arrive on the same day that Doug and Pierre meet. They are consulted, and they support the idea. Doug is an exceptional trainer and would be the one to pull this off. Pierre Grunstein agrees to the plan. The trainer is beaming with pride. The associate producer turns over to Doug the two brown bear cubs that were in the care of the German trainer Dieter Kraml. Doug immediately gives them English names: "Ben" and "Bonnie." Informed of the changes, Jean-Jacques approves the decision. Should the training succeed, he will have at his disposal a hitherto unimaginable asset. Moreover, it will be the first time in history that a large bear will have been trained alongside an unrelated cub.

Starting on the following day, Doug divides the training tasks. He has Bart rehearse movements that are very precise and lets his son-in-law, Clint, take charge of Ben and Bonnie's training before bringing them closer to the adult bear. At four months old, the cubs are still too young to follow orders. A small wooden board sixteen inches by twelve inches called "point" serves as a marker. Tirelessly repeated, the word "point" echoes in their ears like an order. No exercises will be performed as long as the cubs are outside their "point." Clint teaches them very simple movements. They have to stand up, look to their left, look to their right, sit down, lie down. Each movement is rewarded with a cherry dipped in syrup. To teach them to go from one place to the other, Clint uses the sound of a bicycle horn. The cubs, who are very sensitive to sound, make their way toward the source of each sound. In ten days, Ben and Bonnie will have made significant progress and will have eyes for nobody but Clint. For his part, Bart will have spent hours learning how to move his huge mass with a minimum of movement. Then the bear and the cubs will be able to meet.

For days, a meeting of an entirely different sort has been taking place a thousand feet away from the infernal mud hole. Despite the icy-cold winds, the crew is very excited about the sequence just shot. The script reads: *Kaar wants to seduce a female bear, Iskwao. Youk watches them.* Forty-foot-high pine trees, clumps of bushes, a broken stump, hundreds of rhododendrons and forget-me-nots have been laid out and planted to create a more attractive landscape. Jean-Jacques, who for a long time has subscribed to the motto "Almighty nature orders seduction above all things," has introduced Grizz to the crew. Four years earlier he had decided to give the role of Iskwao, Kaar's girlfriend, to Grizz. "Her" silvery fur reflects the sun's rays and "her" clear, smooth face highlights beautiful eyes. The technicians are enchanted by "her." Enchanting Doc, however, is more important. Mark Wiener has made certain that the bears enter the meadow from opposite ends and that each is separated from

Doug Seus trains Bart, while Clint Youngreen trains Bonnie. It will be the first time in history that a large bear will have been trained alongside an unrelated cub.

Two months later, the results
are spectacular.

the other by hot wires. The irony is that these two bears, both of whom have been raised by the same trainer, merely share the same roof; they do not live together. They cannot stand each other. The director of photography asks the trainer to wait for better light before allowing the bears onto the scene, so that the entrance of the lovers can be more magnificent. The lovers observe one another from afar, falsely casual. Grizz nears the stump under which Varin has placed thousands of ants and swallows them up while staring at Doc.

In reply to this provocation, the script calls for Kaar to hurl a large rock in order to impress the beautiful female. This rock has been a source of worry for Toni Ludi, the production designer, and his assistants. For three weeks, part of the special-effects crew has slaved over its construction. It has to be light so that it is easy to transport—three hundred pounds at the very most— and yet solid enough to withstand Doc's fifteen hundred pounds. Moreover, it has to blend with the landscape. All set designers know that rocks are the most difficult natural objects to copy.

The storyboard sequence for the lovemaking scene between Kaar and Iskwao.

About to start filming the scene, Jean-Jacques is surprised at the result of so much labor. Made of polyester covered with cement, the rock looks rather dull and artificial. Nonetheless, they have to continue filming.

Action! "Push, Doc, push," shouts the trainer. The bear follows his orders so well that he tips over the rock. Surprised at finding so little resistance, he leans over the edge of the cliff, impressed by his own exploit. There follows a low-angle shot.

Between takes, Jean-Jacques takes out his tape recorder and dictates a memo to the editor: "Use very little of this take, only a few seconds, that's all." Then he goes looking for Doc, who, on Mark's orders, has left his tree stump and wandered off onto the plain. Sexy, provocative, erotic, coquettish, Grizz casts mischievous glances and assumes vampish postures, doing all "she" can to make certain that Doc is not indifferent to "her" allure. Then, on the trainer's orders, "she" performs a sumptuous backward roll, legs lifted in the air. "Let me remind the cameramen that this young lady is a boy. Be careful to conceal her masculinity," suggests the director.

On Mark Wiener's command, Grizz rolls over.

In Kaar's role, Doc feels out of sorts. He is supposed to pursue his fiancée. However, one of the most difficult things in training a bear is getting him to run on command. The Kodiak curses, growls, grumbles. The film director asks Mark Wiener to liven up his bear. The trainer laughs. The bears are so well trained that Jean-Jacques expects them to react in increasingly more controllable ways. But Doc wants no part of it.

The trainer finally decides on a possible solution. With a box of marshmallows in one hand and a bucket of chicken in the other, he sprints past the bear, displaying the delicacies. Everyone bursts out laughing. Doc starts out with a sluggish lope, but once he speeds up, he does not stop. "Faster, Mark, faster; you're in the frame," Jean-Jacques shouts.

The trainer is breathless. Doc approaches, and Mark, exhausted, takes cover behind a tree. Being extremely nearsighted, as most bears are, Doc keeps running straight past him. The director is overjoyed. Now it's Grizz's turn. The same happens, followed by the same burst of laughter. Changing direction, Mark runs past Grizz, holding a bright blue cooler. Lured by the noise, the bear keeps trying to catch up. Mark is the quicker of the two, until he trips. Grizz falls half on top of him, grabs the cooler, and, like a cat, hides in the bushes.

Toward the end of the day the director reviews the scenes he has shot. Everything has gone well. Still missing are the lovemaking scenes. It is impossible to bring together Doc and Grizz. There would be carnage. It is already arranged that mimes will act out the scene. The next day, Jean-Jacques announces the departure of "Grizz the actress." The technicians bid the bear good-bye by applauding. She—that is, he—has been a source of delight.

Everyone wakes up at 5:30 A.M. in order to leave at 6:15 A.M. Filming a scene takes longer, now that the days are shorter. Of all the technicians, Xavier is always the first to arrive on the film set. He loves to breathe the silence that lingers on the empty set and the odor of fresh coffee brought to him by the canteen woman. While he is drinking, he thinks of the difficulties to be encountered in the scene they will be filming in a few hours. For today *Kaar will embrace Iskwao*. Or, more precisely, Baldwyn, wearing Kaar's fake skin, will hug Roman Stefanski, wearing Iskwao's.

On the meadow of love, the director has a terrible fit. How can one film a love scene with two such lousy actors? The director asks that the bearskins be redone. Ailsa Berk is shattered; the mimes are dismayed. Pierre Grunstein tries in vain to comfort them. Their talent is not being questioned. Once the

storm has passed, the director spends the rest of the day exhausting all possible setups for the scene. In the corner of the frame, Douce's understudy observes the mimes coupling behind the foliage. The cameras film a small shrub, which one of the assistants shakes with all her might. It is one of a number of ways to suggest the sexual act as perceived from Youk's perspective. For what truly interests the director is the look on the cub's face as he observes lovemaking for the first time in his life.

Gérard Brach wrote this scene by digging into his own past. At the age of seven, he walked through a greenhouse window and severly injured both legs. Confined to his bed in the room next to his mother's bedroom, he heard his stepfather arrive. He heard the sound of laughter, of talking; then he heard nothing at all. Through the partition, all he could make out was the sound of panting and sighing and squealing, then, once again, laughter and talking. This memory had long troubled the script writer, who brought it back to life through the astonished eyes with which the young bear watches the adults give themselves over to their "funny gymnastics."

Of course, the director intends to entrust Youk's role in this scene to Douce. The cub arrives. Like a film star who has had her hair and face made up, she gives the film director the wide variety of expressions he wants. Fascinated by this mass of fur that is so talented, Jean-Jacques wishes to film a last

109

surprised look. But Douce has had enough. To get her attention, five or six technicians bustle about the camera, bang on canvas sheets, and clap their hands. Douce watches them with ironic distance. She is beginning to learn the tricks of the trade. Then Jean-Jacques starts to howl like a dog baying at the moon, and the crew joins in. The cub, intrigued, looks to the right, then to the left. It works!

Douce is sick. While adult bears are busy conquering one another, Youk has settled in front of a patch of mushrooms, which he sniffs and chews on to relieve his boredom. Using a foam base, the decorators have done their job well. They have planted large red mushrooms with white spots, each with a different taste. Some taste like honey, others like almond paste, and still others like Jell-O, fish, and chicken. Douce has shown a decided preference for fish and almond-paste mushrooms. After each take the nursemaids attempt to separate the cub from the mushrooms. The cub has so stuffed herself that she's developed a liver condition. Snuggled up in the arms of her "mother," who is pale with worry, the cub shivers and trembles.

Douce has eaten so many mushrooms that she comes down with an upset stomach.

As soon as veterinarian François Hugues is informed, he arrives on the first flight from Paris. After taking a stool sample and administering intestinal antiseptics, he wraps her up in blankets. On the set, Jean-Jacques asks about her hourly and, after filming, goes to have a little chat with her. Douce scampers about as usual and has resumed her human face.

Love in the meadow is practically over. What remains to be filmed, once Kaar's and Iskwao's artificial skins are remade, is the actual love scene itself. The overall impression generated by this scene is one of gaiety and fantasy.

Tomorrow they will start a new scene, beginning a different part of the film, and only Jean-Jacques and Xavier are aware of its extreme complexity.

Thursday, June 18: It is the twenty-sixth day of filming and the first day of the second month. The anniversary is celebrated in hail and cold.

Through San Martino, headed toward Cavallera, the minibuses trundle their way through a muddy path littered with stones. After three miles they stop. The crew wades through the mud to explore the new location. At an altitude of eighty-two hundred feet, it is an exposed, windy plateau surrounded by immense, jagged mountains. In order to reach it, the technicians must climb on foot for one mile on an incline of 650 feet. Collapsing under the weight of their equipment, they are no longer smiling. This is to be the scenery for the opening sequence of the film. Filming was originally supposed to begin here, but it had to be postponed until the snow melted.

The script reads: *"On that day, in an imposing landscape, daubed by bright colors of Spring, the sun is nearing its high point. A mother bear, followed by her bear cub, Youk, is working her way through the crack of a rock at the foot of a tree. She is stuffing herself with honey she has unearthed. Youk rushes to claim as much honey as he can with his tiny pink tongue from the lips of his mother. The mother bear forages once again between the rocks. Alas, an enormous boulder perched above her is shaken loose and comes crashing down. Youk barely has time to move away, but his mother is crushed. What has happened? The cub does not understand why his mother does not move. Time passes. Helpless, tired, Youk falls asleep snuggling up to his mother, who is forever motionless."*

The director knows that this is one of the most delicate scenes to film. First of all, the existing weather conditions are hardly those described in the script. The weather is horrible. Jean-Jacques, however, would like the viewer to experience, from the very first frame, a feeling of natural beauty and romantic landscape.

For the scenes depicting the closeness between the mother bear and her cub, he will use the German bear belonging to Alfons Spindler, along with her two cubs. The scenes with the mother by herself will be played by the twins of Dieter Kraml. Finally, the scenes in which the mother bear is crushed by the falling rock will be played by Ailsa Berk. As for Youk, he will be played at times by Gogol. By using three mother bears, three cubs, and a mime, Jean-Jacques hopes to convey a wide range of emotions: tenderness, cheerfulness, tension, sadness, forgetting, and the return to life—an almost impossible balance, to which for several weeks he has given much thought.

Before placing the cameras, he explains his intentions in detail to the cameramen. Technically, they will have to be extremely rigorous and move from extreme close-ups—nose to nose—to wide-angle shots that reach to the very borders of perception. Philippe Rousselot listens, while noticing that the fog has become so thick that the scenery has become invisible.

Nothing is filmed all morning. In the canteen, located about a mile downhill, the atmosphere is morose. The meal lasts until the middle of the afternoon. A thick white sheet of mist surrounds the tent. At 4:00 P.M. the director, to motivate the technicians, suggests a walk through the scenery, just to exercise their limbs. At 6:00, without a foot of film shot, it's time to wrap.

The German trainer Alfons Spindler with one of the bears who will play the part of Youk's mother, along with her cubs, one of which will play the very young Youk.

Friday, June 19: by 6:30 A.M., in every room, the occupants are going through the same motions. They draw the double curtains and cast despairing looks outside. The fog is everywhere, unbearable, pounding against the windows.

Nevertheless, an hour later, the minibus begins to stir. Philippe, Arnaud, and Michele cover their cameras in large canvas bags, which the crew stuffs with sacks of rice to keep the humidity away. With his light meter pointed at the sky, the director of photography is growing increasingly pessimistic. He picks up a large stone and hands it to his assistant: "Could you hold this while I fix something? I'll only be a minute." It's a trick Philippe unfailingly plays on his assistants on days when ill humor prevails.

Yet another wasted day. Pierre goes back to his expense ledger. The budget is swelling dangerously. It has reached $20 million. To calm himself, the associate producer goes around telling everyone: "It's going to be hard, very hard, until the beginning of August."

The crew shivers. After filming each day, Jean-Jacques forces himself to take some time alone to reflect. Increasingly, he enjoys taking a long walk, ten to twelve miles, sometimes to find a quiet restaurant, where he dines by himself, a fork in one hand and the storyboards in the other. For this sequence, more than for any other in the film, it is vital that he think of the filming and the editing simultaneously.

Saturday, June 20: wake-up is at 5:00 A.M. Xavier moves the schedule forward, hoping that the early morning will be better than the afternoon, but the sky remains gray and rain looms. The crew sets up as quickly as possible. With the walkie-talkie, Isabelle, the second assistant, calls the trainer Dieter Kraml from the canteen and asks him to bring his ravishing twins for the scene *The mother bear digs in search of honey.*

Next to a huge rock, the set designers have planted a dead tree, and, between its roots, have dug a hole through the rock, which is now ready to receive a swarm of bees. The director explains in English to a technician the movements that one of the twins is expected to perform. The technician translates the instructions into German for the trainer. With his inscrutable face, protruding canines, steely hands, and boxer's build, Kraml is a unique spectacle. After listening and thinking, he presses both his thick index fingers to his temples and says, "Difficult, very difficult. Ziz iz my zinking."

Isabelle hands out beekeepers' suits before Varin releases the bees and a honeycomb. Action! It starts to rain. They wait. The shower stops. Varin

The German trainer Dieter Kraml with another bear who also plays the role of Youk's mother.

brings more honey to the bees. One of the twins takes her place. Action! Three takes. The director is not satisfied. They are random shots, of no interest.

In the afternoon, Jean-Jacques summons the other trainer, Alfons Spindler, his female bear, and her two cubs. This bear is far less attractive than Kraml's twins. The cameramen will have to outdo themselves, and the make-up artist, Hans, will have to perform miracles to give the illusion of continuity between the bears. .

Armed with spray-paint cans containing silver, gold, and light yellow, Hans creates a double. Needless to say, it takes a lot of time. Spindler becomes first impatient, then furious. His anger reaches its peak when Xavier asks him to remove the bear's muzzle so they can shoot the scene. Unable to read the script, this circus man has no idea of what the plot entails. Why should he remove a bright-red muzzle? A volley of abuse reaches the ears of the assistant director. Pierre gets involved and explains the situation succinctly: "With muzzle, no money!" This Spindler understands. Two minutes later, the bear is ready to be filmed. Jean-Jacques asks the trainer to hide one of his two cubs so that they can film the scene. Again, there's an argument. "Never. Either both, or neither," he replies.

Pierre, once again, is on the spot. Spindler removes one of the twins from the set, but places him in full view of his mother eight feet away. Action! The abandoned cub, crying, runs to his mother and his twin. In the space of a few seconds, everything falls apart. The bear runs toward the cameras and then up the mountain. Helped by Kraml, Spindler attempts to get her back, but, as though she has gone mad, she flees, performing somersaults on the way, her cubs hard on her heels. The crew is glued to their spots, petrified, except for Isabelle, who tries to cut off her path.

"Stop, Evel Knievel, will you?" shouts Rousselot. At any rate, the protective barrier stops the bear. But no one feels like smiling. Not a single foot of film has been shot in two days, and today these trainers who were unable to control their beasts have caused a lot of time to be wasted. The director demands that Kraml and Spindler stay on the set after filming so they can rehearse with their bears for tomorrow's scene.

Monday, June 22: wake-up is at 5:00 A.M. With puffy eyes, the crew sets out on the road to Cavallera. Sensing that Jean-Jacques is not in a joking mood, the German trainers are already on the set for the sequence *Youk stands next to her mother, who is searching for honey.* The morning starts out with Gogol playing Youk and Ailsa Berk in the role of the mother bear, so that Kraml and Spindler—whom Pierre Grunstein has dubbed "Professor Spindler of the University of Heidelberg"—can gain an understanding of the plot.

The fake bearskin worn by the mime is resilient and very well made. It resembles the skin of the twins. The illusion is perfect. Ailsa puts on the costume and settles between the rocks. By walkie-talkie Jean-Jacques tells her what to do: "Start fidgeting a bit, Ailsa; make as many movements as you can with your paws. Grab the honey. But what's wrong with this honey? It's pitch black. Varin, find me another kind of honey, either acacia or wild melon honey, as long as it's golden honey."

"Most people think that honeycombs are golden, but their real color is dark brown," replies Varin.

"Then I'm like most people too. Besides, the color gold looks better in films," says the director, upset. "Ailsa, go ahead. Chase the bees away. Careful, Gogol is coming closer. Take out the honeycomb. Give it to the cub. Cut! It's fantastic."

Back to Kraml's twins: but where has their trainer gone? He has disappeared. By walkie-talkie, Xavier asks his whereabouts, and locates him in the canteen. He has already drunk quite a bit in the company of his comrade,

For the scene with the bees, Annaud dons a mosquito-netting hat.

"Professor Spindler." The first assistant goes downhill to fetch Kraml, and, dragging him by his shirt collar, brings him back.

The technicians put on their beekeepers' suits. Jean-Jacques puts on a lovely anti-mosquito hat, a solar topee to which is attached a stiff veil of very fine mesh, which makes him look like a distinguished lady. One of the twins takes her place. Action!

"Cut! Well done, Kraml," comments Jean-Jacques. The trainer all too hastily draws the conclusion that the day's filming is over. Suddenly aware of the inflatable swimming pool, which serves as a reservoir, he pushes in his twins and, to impress everyone, throws himself in after them. He comes out dripping wet, breaks into coarse laughter, and goes downhill to the canteen to warm up with some apple brandy.

Jean-Jacques announces: "O.K. I'm ready. Let's proceed." Everyone is dismayed. Tentatively Xavier relates the incident. Jean-Jacques becomes tense. "Very well. Tell 'Professor Spindler' to come uphill with his bears."

The message is transmitted. The answer is fast and categorical: the "Professor" will come uphill provided he is accompanied by Kraml. And Kraml

116

can accompany him only on condition that he may dry himself first. Jean-Jacques turns to Pierre: "Can you intercede?"

Ten minutes later, the crackpots are in place on the rocks. "Action! Michele, focus on the mother and then come around to the cub. Look, they're eating together; it's fantastic. Arnaud, close in on the cub."

Philippe closes in on the mother. Varin releases some more bees. The animal consultant shakes his beehive the second Kraml and Spindler advance. The bees surround the German trainers, who have refused to protect themselves. The insects infiltrate their clothes and tangle themselves in their hair. They scream, jump about like kids, and tear down the incline, ripping off their shirts and anoraks in front of a crew that is bursting with laughter. Jean-Jacques wonders when and if he will ever reach the end of this sequence.

"I am ready," he says dryly. " 'Professor Spindler,' place some honey on the mother's snout. No, not on the cub's mouth. Wipe that off. Action!" The cub laps up the nectar with delight. The intimacy between the cub and his mother is compelling. Suddenly the crew is quiet, moved by the sight.

Tuesday, June 23: since 7:00 A.M. the clouds have been threatening rain. Sequence: *On a rock, Youk looks at his mother grabbing honey.* The cameramen cover their cameras with canvas sheets, and the technicians huddle together in a tent and wait.

As the cub licks the honey from its mother's lips, it is an emotional moment for the members of the crew.

"Break lunch," proposes Xavier in pidgin English. In the canteen, the mood is down and the jokes are bland. Jean-Jacques keeps coming and going, examining the sky. At 3:00 P.M. he shouts, "It's blue. Let's go."

At once the crew gets up, trundles through the mud, removes the canvas covering the camera, and repeats the scene. Half an hour later, the damned fog is covering up the set again while hail pelts the cameras. Once again the crew takes cover in a tent. Pierre, who becomes a cynic in extreme situations, exclaims, "I think the first year will be the hardest."

Xavier, Jean-Jacques, and Philippe, who have stayed on the set, enter the tent.

"Pierre, we've just filmed five scenes."

"For this film?"

"Five shots of clouds," adds Jean-Jacques sadly.

The location manager charges into the tent, saying, "The stags have just arrived. Varin, you should go see them."

The road is narrow and bumpy, which makes it difficult for the trucks to climb to the set. The owner of the stags, who two days earlier had left Normandy, where he owns a fifty-acre park, leads a herd of two hundred stags. Since this is the first time he has lent his stags to the film industry, he decided to accompany them personally. Varin sets up a three-thousand-square-foot enclosure. A huge storm breaks out. The day is ruined.

Wednesday, June 24: the sun rises but there is no dawn. The cameras take turns filming clouds and the expressions on Youk's face.

"Rebuild this scenery, it's horrible. We're in the middle of nature here, not in a studio," shouts Jean-Jacques. "Meanwhile, we'll have lunch." On the way he meets Varin's defeated gaze.

"Problems, Jean-Philippe?"

"Yes. A big one. One of the stags has run away."

"When?"

"Last night. He cut through the net."

"Which stag was it?"

"One of the big ones. You know, when things go wrong, they . . ."

"Any chance of finding it?"

"None. He went down the valley. By this time he's probably almost at Venice." The director does not move. His fits of repressed anger are worse than when he yells.

At 3:00 P.M. filming resumes. "Let's get started; the light is good. If we wait any longer, it will rain."

"Jean-Jacques, wait; we still haven't finished adjusting the scenery as you asked."

"That's my responsibility! I don't give a damn about the scenery," retorts the director, who hardly means what he says. "If we wait any longer, we'll lose the light. Just plant some more grass."

A set designer walks toward the tree, a tuft in his hand. "Wait," shouts Xavier. "Varin has just put the bees in it." It is too late. The insects suddenly swarm up and attack the man. In the space of a few seconds, his neck swells. Dazed, he stumbles on a stone and falls flat on the ground.

"Well, are we ready?" shouts Jean-Jacques, more concerned with lighting than with the state of the designer. But mist descends upon the valley, concealing bushes and buttercups. The production shuts down, and everyone returns to their hotel. When they arrive at San Martino, a storm of unbelievable power breaks out and cloaks the whole area in darkness.

Jean-Jacques's mother has just arrived. She has come to celebrate her eightieth birthday with her only son. Eight days later, when she is about to leave, she addresses the crew with these sweet words: "You know, my son has always been a source of enduring satisfaction for me."

Thursday, June 25: same schedule. The sky is now touching the ground, which is flooded from the rain. In order to appease the heavenly forces, Jean-Jacques and Philippe begin chanting, "O Jerusalem beata." The chorus is so sinister that they burst out laughing. They must film whatever the cost. "Let's film the scene in which the mother bear is crushed by the mass of falling rocks," suggests the director at the height of despair.

For three whole hours, at the top of the rock in front of which the dead tree has been planted, the set-design team piles dozens of rocks and sets up the device that will trigger the avalanche.

"Let's start filming. We'll see how it turns out. Xavier, as soon as you hear the whistle, pull the cable. Action! Go ahead; release it!"

"The falling rocks are fantastic," exclaims Jean-Jacques a few seconds later. He immediately verifies on the video screen whether his joyful exclamation reflects satsifaction at having filmed anything at all or whether it reflects a truly good shot. He is sufficiently pleased not to ask for a second take. Finally, this day, which boded nothing good, has furnished him with a take.

Friday, June 26: The crew curses the rocks and re-creates the sequence, which has now taken eight days. *The cub does not understand that his mother does not move.* The British team place an empty skin under the fallen rocks. Next to the dead tree, the film director himself arranges the rocks that fell the day before. Action! Suddenly the sun appears, an incongruous, unaccustomed sight.

"Oh, damn," says Philippe. "Even when it's nice it's lousy. Now we need it to become gray or at least overcast, so it matches the other takes."

This morning, Philippe has had enough; he has not even shaved. Leaning against his camera, he dozes and waits. Ever since filming began, the weather has granted the dimmest of lighting. All of his conversations with Jean-Jacques lead to one conclusion: that they must concentrate on scenes in which something powerful takes place rather than those with less intensity, with the rationale that these will blend in with one another on a conceptual level.

Nevertheless, Philippe would still prefer that there be a semblance of meteorological consistency. His work in this film has not been easy. First there were the limitations caused by the location of the cameras. Then they had to wait for the installation of electrical wires and animatronics. Then they had to take into account the time needed to explain things to the trainers as well as to rehearse the animals. Only then could Philippe make decisions based on aesthetic concerns. Although he knows that the credibility of each scene is more important than the lighting, and that a director of photography should not be out to change the world, still he exclaims in a fury, "This is like reporting from Beirut: one shouldn't be waiting for light."

"How much time do you need to get ready?" asks Xavier.

"Your question really annoys me. I've been ready for two hours." And yet, with his light meter, he gauges the sky. "It's good now, but it will be gray in five seconds. Let's go."

At this precise moment, from the top of the mountain, joyously making their way downhill, with their bells pealing, a flock of about a hundred sheep is headed directly toward the rock. "Oh, no," shouts Jean-Jacques. Xavier, can you push them back?"

Yes, Xavier can do anything, even hold off a flock of sheep.

"Let's start, Jean-Jacques," adds Philippe. "It's fine."

"Varin, place Gogol next to the mime's skin," says the director. "Oh, damn: the bees. What are they doing? Too bad, we'll shoot anyway. No,

Gogol, don't roll up the fur. Quickly, could someone please put it back in its place? Quick, quick, or we'll end up with nothing again."

"What a mess up there," remarks Philippe, his head turned toward the sky. "Let's try anyway."

"I'm sorry. It's too late," says the director, a touch of exasperation in his voice.

Filming resumes in half an hour. Gogol misses his entrance and runs to hide behind Michele's movable platform. "Cut! Let's take it again. Action!"

This time, the cub is fantastic. He comes closer to the motionless fur, clutches it with his paw, shakes it as if to play, then lets it fall again, motionless. Standing up, he strains to remove the rocks, sits down, turns around toward the cameras, and offers an unforgettable expression, one that everyone will later swear having seen: sorrow.

"Magnificent," says Jean-Jacques. "These animals are extraordinary." Despite the complexities of the situation, the pieces of the puzzle fit together, and the sequence draws to a close.

Saturday, June 27: veterinarian François Hugues arrives at the canteen with his plastic surgeon's instruments. Five days earlier, Douce had been taken to the English crew's studio to help the make-up artists match the color of the Youk animatronic's fur to her own. Not being used to luxury hotels, she smashed into a glass door. The enormous blow wounded her beautiful muzzle. Despite ointment applied by the local veterinarian, it remains swollen. François Hugues tranquilizes her and lays her down on a table. Gingerly he irrigates the wound to reduce the risk of infection. Xavier arrives.

"Hi, handsome."

"Hi, Doc. Do you think you'll be able to reduce the swelling?"

"Yes."

"By the way, how is Prince Rainier's rhinoceros?"

"I'm going there on July fourteenth. I'll let you know."

The operation lasts fifteen minutes. To prevent the cub from opening up the wound while scratching, and infecting herself, Dr. Hugues takes out of his case a sturdy white collar that looks like a lampshade and fastens it around her neck. Douce looks like a nun. She must wear the veil for five days, but her grumpiness when she wakes up does not speak well for her vocation.

Monday, June 29: the tenth and last day at Cavallera is used for the final close-ups of Gogol being greedy, happy, helpless, astonished, tired—as many expressions as the scene requires.

Xavier leaves the set to walk François to Mark Wiener's house. His bear Grizz was unable to sleep all night because of a very bad toothache. The pain is such that he has become hysterical and unapproachable. Curled up at the edge of his cage, he even refuses to admit his trainer. Helped by a local dentist, the veterinarian puts the bear to sleep. They must hurry, because the anesthesia lasts no more than half an hour. Nine people take Grizz out of his cage, while the doctor prepares his instruments. Upon opening the mouth of the colossus, he finds the cause of the trouble: a huge cavity.

Xavier serves as interpreter. "Does Mark want to a denture put in?" asks the veterinarian.

"Yes, but in Los Angeles. Just treat the infection for now."

Fascinated, the dentist takes his first look at a bear's teeth. When the production company placed an urgent call to a dental clinic in Fiera di Primiero,

Bart and Bonnie

panic swept through the office on hearing the nature of the patient. He was the first to offer his services. The procedure, which is quick and meticulous, lasts no more than fifteen minutes. Having inspected the other teeth, the dentist sharpens a molar with the help of a mason's file.

"Mark asks if you could manicure the claws," Xavier says to François. "That's no problem," he replies. François cuts the claws and touches them up with a file. The beauty treatment is finished. Grizz is returned to his cage, which Mark covers up with a black sheet.

Tomorrow Grizz will fly back to the United States, accompanied by Mark's fiancée. The trainer is hoping that the filming will be finished soon, for he is to be married in September and has already informed the production company that he will under no circumstances postpone the ceremony. Each day, he laughs as he repeats to whomever will listen to him, "I don't want to miss my wedding. Damn movie!"

After climbing down from their rock for the last time, Jean-Jacques, Pierre, and Philippe get into the car, and on their way to San Martino they start an unusual conversation.

"You know, Jean-Jacques, I visited Doug Seus. He is a truly remarkable trainer. When I arrived, Bart and the cub were crawling about three feet from each other."

"Then the sequence of the stag chase, in which Kaar initiates Youk into hunting, stands a good chance of being magnificent," comments Jean-Jacques, who is delighted.

"Regarding this sequence, Doug Seus gave me a sketch suggesting ideal spots for you to place the cameras," whispers Pierre while taking a sheet of paper out of his pocket.

The director gets angry. "I'll place my cameras where I please. Nobody is going to decide that for me."

"For the shot in which Kaar and Youk devour the stag, the trainer suggests that we stuff the inside of the carcass with cooked meat mixed with marsh-mallows," continues Pierre timidly.

"Out of the question," retorts Jean-Jacques. "I've spent an entire meal with him explaining that I do not want cooked meat and sweets. I want raw meat so that the scene will be more realistic." Silence. Jean-Jacques continues: "We had this discussion in 1984. For three years now I've refused to have marsh-mellows in the meat." Between hiccups, Philippe chuckles. "It's really the first time I've heard of a film director having these kinds of problems."

Shut up in her editing room in Paris, Noëlle Boisson sits in front of the rushes like a child at a puppet show. For a month and a half, day in and day out, she has sat there being constantly surprised. She too is fascinated by the wealth of expressions on the bears' faces, by the variety of feelings they convey on film. They have a lot to offer, but she must create some order out of the enormous amount of exposed film. Frame after frame, she sifts through images that fit precisely into the plot as detailed by the script. Then there is all the extra footage, those exceptional moments that the cameras captured during filming. Noëlle not only wants to create a plausible narrative sequence, but must also interpret what she discovers and decipher the feelings that a particular expression or posture on the part of the animal conveys.

She views and reviews the rushes, which she practically knows by heart, to understand better the staging options as well as the positions of the cameras. Then begins the process of filing, sorting, and itemizing. There are frames whose place in the story is easily identifiable. Then there are frames that do not relate to a specific scene but may eventually be used someplace in the story. Thus, Noëlle has created her own self-contained *cinémathèque* (film library), where she stores images of a posture, an expression, a gesture made by Youk, Kaar, or the others, which she might want to draw on later.

In the editing room in Paris, Noëlle Boisson is fascinated by the images she discovers.

It is a colossal job involving very detailed archival work. But it is very gratifying work as well. For the first time in her sixteen years as a film editor, Noëlle is editing a film in which ninety percent of the story is told without words. Without the traditional reference points provided by dialogue, but instead having before her only images that must themselves speak, she at times feels as though she has returned to the early days of cinema. It is a magical sensation. Unforeseen interpretations suggest themselves. And the only question is how to put them together.

This question, in fact, has been hovering over the film's location for quite some time. How will the scenes Jean-Jacques has filmed in short snatches be organized in a fluid and coherent manner? Only he knows, and yet . . . Indeed, each individual scene in the script is physically possible to film, provided one has incorporated all the necessary visual subterfuges, camouflages, stratagems, and tricks. In *The Bear* nature plays a leading role from beginning to end. Yet, paradoxically, it is also a film in which the least natural means must constantly be used. In the field, the purpose of the imagination is primarily to find solutions to problems that no one could have anticipated.

Who, for example, could have predicted that Kaar and Youk's encounter with the herd of stags would turn into such an absolute headache? Without a doubt, a stag is one of the most difficult animals in the world to tame. For an entire day, ten people exhaust themselves trying to chase four stags into a defined area, an area Jean-Jacques has chosen because the cameras will be able to film them against wonderful backlighting. How do they get the stags to pass through the narrow gully where the cameramen were waiting for them? To many, this feat seems nothing less than a miracle. The incident convinces the director that the remainder of the sequence will require the same tricks outlined by the storyboards.

The next day, therefore, a twenty-year-old man who lives nearby takes the place of one of the stags. He is reputed to be an ace on a motorcycle, which is why he is hired. On his shoulders the crew places a beautiful stag's head with antlers made of resin—manufactured by the set designers. Then he speeds as fast as possible along the very bumpy path. One camera films the stag's antlers in profile, through a screen of ferns, while the other focuses on the fake head from the movable platform. During rehearsals, the motorcyclist charges down the prescribed path and performs the task perfectly. It's much more difficult, of course, to reproduce the scene with *Kaar pursuing one of the stags;* that is, with Doc running after a motorcycle. And Doc is having a bad day.

Filmed through the foliage at a steep angle, this expert motorcyclist will simulate a fleeing stag.

He simply refuses to run. His trainer, Mark, tries all sorts of lures—running between the rails of the movable platform and acting out the scene, shouting, whispering words of encouragement—but nothing helps. Doc leaps sluggishly, is out of breath, stops, starts, and stops again. In the space of a few seconds, he has run about ten yards.

On the third day, Jean-Jacques decides to add an additional piece to his build-it-yourself stag: hooves. In reality, they will be a horse's hooves. The director has a camera tied under the belly of a stallion, aimed between the hooves. The rider is to activate the camera with the help of a rope tucked under his saddle as soon as he feels the bear against the horse's hindquarters. It is a rather clever idea, but from the very first take the rider panics and messes everything up. Not only do his hands tremble so badly that he is unable to activate the camera, but he communicates his fear to the horse, who begins to shy and to dodge out of the frame. Since Doc is no more valiant today than he was yesterday, one can sympathize with the director's exasperation at the end of the day.

At any rate, the scene is not yet complete, since it lacks its most essential shot: the one in which the bear attacks the stag. How can one create this illusion? The director comes up with an idea: to have Doc run straight toward the camera. When he is three feet away from the camera, someone will throw him something so that he will have to grab it. This will give the impression that he is lunging at the stag.

It is no sooner said than done. Standing on his hind legs the bear charges Arnaud's camera. Mark throws him an apple. Doc immediately seizes it with his front paws. After the third attempt, the director is satisfied. During editing, by adding a fraction of a second to this frame, one should be able to see the attack gesture. Half a day's work for a usable fraction of a second. Did you say patience?

This hardworking routine, this path filled with unexpected obstacles, this thankless craft sown daily with pitfalls, in short, this inglorious filming would, toward the middle of July, experience its moment of grace. The script reads:

Mark Wiener gets Doc to look like he's attacking.

127

Kaar initiates Youk into the hunt. Lying on the ground, they observe the stags. For weeks, Doug Seus has been training Bart and Bonnie. It seems that he has performed wonders in bringing the two closer together. The trainer himself tells everyone that he is ready to prove himself in front of the cameras. Jean-Jacques decides that this will be the scene.

That morning, Doug and his son-in-law, Clint, arrive on the film set in an obvious state of excitement. They are impatient to get started. While the technical crew is setting up, Doug with Bart and Clint with Bonnie rehearse for the last time. Everyone in the crew watches from the corner of his eyes, looking for the reactions of the bear and the cub to each other. Everything appears calm. And then, at noon, Jean-Jacques begins rolling. Out of shot, Doug looks at Bart, who is standing up, monumental. Clint does the same with Bonnie, minuscule. At this instant, in this lost corner of the Dolomites, absolute silence reigns. Everyone holds his breath, as 150 pairs of eyes are riveted on the two immobile animals.

Softly, Doug says, "Bart, down. Don't move."

In the same tone of voice, Clint says, "Bonnie, down. Don't move."

Then, as if by magic, Bart flattens himself against the ground. Bonnie does likewise. The trainers keep their eyes riveted on their animals.

"Let's start," murmurs Jean-Jacques, "and let no one make a sound."

With their voices separated a tenth of a second, Doug and Clint speak the same command: "Crawl."

Slowly, the bear and the cub, both flat on the grass, side by side, begin to crawl. Suddenly Bart lifts his hindquarters, and, sure enough, Bonnie imitates him, in perfect synchronization. It is an extraordinary moment charged with overpowering emotion. Jean-Jacques has tears in his eyes. What he is witnessing is nothing more nor less than the theme of his film: the friendship between a bear and a cub, one taking the other under his care. This duo, which would have been impossible in nature, is performing "for real," without tricks or artifice, in front of three cameras. Indeed, it is a beautiful moment, in which cinema is compounded by a first in the history of animal training. The seconds move slowly. Everyone knows that the scene will be magnificent. "Cut," shouts Annaud. Turning to the trainers, he adds, "That was extraordinary. Congratulations."

After the emotion comes the euphoria. Both Americans run toward their animals. Bart embraces Doug and scratches Doug's bare back. But the trainer, it seems, feels no pain. Exultantly he kisses the bear on the muzzle and thanks

Trained to crawl simultaneously in this scene, Bart and Bonnie make their first appearance together on the film set.

The cub mimics the grown bear—a true moment of grace during the filming.

him, almost stammering. As for Clint, he offers Bonnie the ultimate reward: a can of candied cherries.

For the director, what has just happened opens up fantastic prospects. If it is possible to have the bear and cub work together, many of the scenes will acquire additional power and authenticity. This represents a qualitative leap for the film.

The next day the film director goes to see Bart. But as though the sky wished to signal that the party was over after two days of sunlight and warmth, fog and rain appear once again. The set becomes a mossy undergrowth invaded by heather and dotted with large red flowers.

Two set designers stuff pounds of meat and yards of intestines into the carcass of a fake stag, which they then sprinkle with a syrupy red liquid. Today's scene is: *Kaar and Youk have a feast.* Bonnie does not need to be asked twice to plunge with gusto into the bloody meat. She digs into the carcass up to her shoulders. But Bart is sulking. He does not even look at the feast. Ten times, twenty times the trainer urges him to imitate the cub. All in vain.

130

It's a bad day. Jean-Jacques Annaud ends the session abruptly: Doc will replace Bart.

The next day, it is the same sequence and the same scenery. Doc, in his turn, is also on a hunger strike. He, at least, has an indisputable excuse: in the carcass he has sniffed out the odor of his fellow bear, and he won't go near it. It is a law of nature. A storm of unusual violence transforms this attempt into a disaster. Maybe there is another solution: call back Bart. But, as should have been expected, the same cause produces the same results. He sniffs out Doc's odor and flees the accursed carcass.

Faced with a situation as absurd as it is unresolvable, Jean-Jacques for the first time feels powerless. So does Doug Seus. Out of ideas, he asks the crew for help. They suggest he speak softly to his bear, put him at ease. It is a strange spectacle to see several technicians treating a two-thousand-pound bear like a capricious baby and begging him as affectionately as possible to eat his meat. One can believe that Bart really needed this show of collective tenderness, because toward the end of the day he finally fastens his mouth onto the mass of bleeding intestines and savors the feast next to the cub, who is insatiable. The director breathes a sigh of relief. He is not the only one to do so. After three days, the sight of the fake blood dripping and of the squalid intestines matted with flies made everyone nauseous, both literally and figuratively. In fact, this was only a preview.

With a six-day-a-week, ten-to-twelve-hour-a-day work schedule, the director has time only on Sundays to step back from his work. After the videocassettes of the rushes filled his room, he moved them to a room on the ground floor. It is there, in what he calls his "private storage room," that Jean-Jacques spends Sundays, organizing his images and his thoughts. With the VCR's remote control in his hand, he scans through scenes on the television screen while making notes into a tape recorder for his editor. His impressions, his intentions, and the new insights he draws from what he sees are secrets he shares with no one except Noëlle Boisson. In fact, no one is authorized to accompany him into this room. Obviously, the members of the crew do not spend their Sundays in the same manner. For Sundays are days of very badly needed rest. They are empty and dull days. Everyone attempts to sleep late, but most are awakened by telephone calls, chambermaids, noises in the corridors. Then they wander around the village hoping to find a newpaper, even if it is out-of-date, in their own languages. Not finding any, most go back to bed. And on Sunday evening, just when everyone is barely beginning to relax, it is time to set the alarm clocks.

At the Vincennes zoo, a man is waiting impatiently for a brown bear to snap out of its lethargic state. François Musy is the engineer in charge of the sound effects for the film. The cage in front of which he is nervously pacing has been completely rearranged according to his specifications. Under a brand-new false ceiling, the walls are covered with wall-to-wall carpeting, behind which microphones have been concealed in four corners. When Maryvonne Leclerc-Cassan, the assistant director of the zoo, places the animal in the cage, it first inspects the premises, then tears out a piece of the rug and quietly lies down on it. This has been going on for an hour, while François paces.

During the five weeks he had spent on location in Italy, he taped reel upon reel of sound material, but the tapes are in a sense still unused. With dialogue nonexistent, sound becomes extremely important because it helps the audience to find its bearings and understand the content of the film. In order for a bear to groan, to growl, or to roar, it has to be provoked. However, one aspect of training a bear consists of teaching it not to make noise.

The trainers were under the impression that sound libraries had a repertoire of all possible sounds emitted by bears. The first assistant director didn't foresee when planning the work schedule that days would be dedicated to sound alone. But the director was experiencing so many difficulties with his own plans that he did not want to push his stars to exhaustion. Everyone in the set had been aware that the film would later be dubbed. Everyone was resigned to this fact except for François Musy. Between scenes he would attempt to tape the "actors." First the cubs—one after the other, they were asked to perform before the microphone. Zazou ran away, Panda cried for half a minute, Gogol was stonily indifferent, and Douce charged the boom operator, then cried for two hours until she was so exhausted she fell asleep. As for the adult bears, the attempt was even briefer. Doug Seus didn't want to have Bart take part in an experiment he considered of no consequence. Still, Doug shoved the microphone at the star's muzzle, and Bart set out to prove that a bear was perfectly capable of placing his lips on a microphone without damaging it. The taping session ended: infuriating.

François then left the location and began touring zoos. At one zoo in Belgium, the owner had just sold his roaring bears. Those he still had were practically mute. In other zoos, the grunting that François elicited was ridiculous. He enlisted the help of the veterinarian François Hugues: "Where else do bears shout?"

"At Vincennes," the doctor replied.

The first attempt is conclusive: at Vincennes the bears do roar, very loudly. But the acoustics are so poor that the tapes are unusable. Then one cage is soundproofed. But the big bear is now sleeping on his piece of rug. Finally, after an hour, he begins to stir. First he gives a weak, tenuous growl. Then the growl becomes a roar, one that grows more and more impressive. After that, it's a festival of bear sounds. An old Persian bear takes over, flying into a rage before giving way to a female grizzly so old that she can emit only a plaintive purr. Finally François has obtained what he wanted. That evening he heads back to Italy.

To reach the new location, it is necessary to leave Cortina d'Ampezzo and travel twenty-five miles while climbing to an altitude of eight thousand feet. Swept by an icy-cold wind, a circle of rocks suddenly appears, like a vestige of a Hollywood film set. Dotted with jutting white crests and surrounded by mountains so high that one's eyes strain to make out their peaks, the sight of Cinque Terre is breathtakingly majestic.

"How beautiful! It's magnificent," remarks Jean-Jacques, his eye glued to the viewfinder of Philippe's camera. But the Italian technicians who toil under the weight of the equipment are of an entirely different opinion. They have only one wish: to abandon this film and return to good, old-fashioned productions in the studios at Cinecittà. They have been on the job forty years, and they couldn't care less about the bears. To them, these daily climbs to rocky peaks are ridiculous, out-of-date, and exhausting.

"I'm cold. I hate this place," grumbles Xavier.

"It's been a month since I last saw rushes," adds Arnaud. "It's hard to work in the dark."

"Come on. Just one short month and a half and it's over" are Pierre's comforting words.

On the terrace of a restaurant located a thousand feet higher up, tourists with binoculars are trying to sight the production's animals. But they are terribly disappointed. Right now the bears are in their cages. All the tourists can distinguish is a pack of ten Doberman pinschers and two men wearing period clothes who do not appear to be technicians.

*Tom is played by the French-
man Tchéky Karyo.*

*Bill is played by the American
Jack Wallace.*

It is now Tuesday, July 28. The filmmakers are about to tackle a pivotal moment in the story: *Two hunters, Tom and Bill, chase Kaar and Youk with a pack of dogs.*

Tom is played by Frenchman Tchéky Karyo, and Bill by the American Jack Wallace. Wearing a gray-green shirt, a leather vest, a linen jacket, and a pair of buff canvas trousers, the French actor buckles around himself a belt fitted with a knife and rifle. Jack is wearing a pair of riding breeches, chaps, a pinkish-beige shirt, and a tobacco-colored vest. Around his hips he wears a holster and a revolver. The costume designer discovered the patterns for these clothes in Canada and had them copied in Paris with fabrics from flea markets and army-navy and tent-cloth suppliers. To give them authenticity, the clothes were discolored by being plunged into numerous dye baths until the ideal aged look was achieved. Each article was then torn, patched, sanded with emery paper, rolled in dirt, rubbed with clay, and soiled with horse and seal fat. When they were ready, their odor was so nauseating, that, out of pity for the actors, the costume designer coated the shirts and pants with Nivea cream.

Out of the cameras' range, Mark Wiener scales the rocky formation next to Doc, Varin's assistants run uphill near Douce, and André Noël unleashes his Dobermans. In the middle of the menagerie, the presence of human actors, on this sixtieth day of filming, is incongruous. Even though they feel comfortable in their hunters' outfits, Tchéky and Jack immediately realize that they have landed on a different planet, where the extraordinary is ordinary. All they can do is try to integrate themselves as best they can, which they have been doing ever since their arrival, ten days earlier, each in his own way. Tchéky already lives the character he portrays with a particular intensity. He hardly ever takes off his costume. To make it look even more worn out he has spent hours climbing and tumbling down rocky slopes. For the past three nights, he has slept in a room he rented at a restaurant high in the mountains, so as to develop a better feel for his role. Early in the morning he goes horseback riding near the circle of rocks, inhaling their odor. For breakfast he eats a piece of dried meat he has been carrying around wrapped in a piece of newspaper he got from the set designers. The date on the newspaper is 1886. To each his own method.

Jack is quite different from Tchéky. He has already toured half the region— "so lovely"—and delighted in pasta—"so divine"—and the fish—"so extraordinary." He sleeps at the hotel and does not inflict upon himself the same sort of physical and psychological punishment as his colleague, whom he finds slightly "mad" but "so real."

"Come on, come on, be a good boy," shouts Mark Wiener. But in the middle of the scene, Doc stalls. A ten-foot rock stands in front of the bear, who cannot find anything on which to place his front paws and lift himself. Sensitive to his trainer's inducements and especially to the smell of chicken wings awaiting him ten feet higher up, the Kodiak begins to struggle upward.

"Xavier, how many chickens for this scene?" asks Jean-Jacques.

"Oh, this scene is worth eight chickens," snickers the first assistant.

Putting one paw in front of the next, Doc makes a last effort, and his fifteen hundred pounds reach the unreachable. Extremely proud of his bear, Mark smiles, too soon.

"Terrific shot. I'm very pleased. Can we do it again for Michele's camera, Mark? You were in the frame," says the director.

Doc is now a distraught colossus. He's got plenty of drive, and he would gladly gulp down a few more chickens, but as far as climbing that same rock

(Right) Doc majestically silhouetted.

Mark Wiener urges Doc to climb a steep slope.

again, it seems inconceivable. He stalls. The director is going to have to make do with the first take.

In the next scene, Douce must follow Doc. But as the script has it, she is supposed to labor at the task. The cub, however, is in Olympic shape, and climbs up in a flash. By the fifth take, when she continues to break all mountain-climbing records, the director shouts, "This won't do at all. Let's find an insurmountable slope."

For the next few days Jean-Jacques moves from one scene to the next. He is working so fast that when he is ready to film the fight between Kaar and the dog pack, Baldwyn, the mime, does not have time to put on his costume properly. It does not matter. The mime, who so far has played his role lying down, motionless, half-concealed behind foliage and rocks, does not want to miss his first opportunity to perform movements before the camera.

Spurred on by André Noël, the dogs attack Baldwyn, who endures the first take in silence but begs Xavier to allow him to mend things before proceeding.

André Lacombe with the pack of Doberman pinschers.

"Jean-Jacques, this is hell for Baldwyn. His head won't stay on, it's a mess," shouts the first assistant.

"That's what movies are about, an accumulation of messes," retorts the director dryly. "It's hard, my dear Baldwyn, but that's your job. Let's take it again."

Action! The dogs hurl themselves on the mime, who falls down like a fly.

"Wait," screams Isabelle, the second assistant. "He lost his feet. He's being bitten everywhere—on his hands, his face."

"Do you need the first-aid kit, Isa?" asks Xavier.

"Well, it's just that . . ."

"Then stay put, and let's carry on," says the director.

"You know, the skin is torn everywhere," insists Isabelle.

"That's fine, that's fine," replies Jean-Jacques.

The mime holds fast for a few seconds, then falls down again.

Jean-Jacques then asks one of André Noël's assistants to put on the skin with which he had trained the dogs to attack. The mime coordinator, Ailsa Berk, has just a few seconds to train him in the rudiments of a bear's movements.

Action! "Stand up straighter; you look like an old man," shouts Jean-Jacques.

The special-effects team is going to be working all night. The next day, Baldwyn's skin looks like an ice-hockey player's uniform. Wrapped in doormat material, his knees padded, his face protected by a helmet, Baldwyn can now let the pack pounce on him all they please.

And where are the hunters during all this? They are present, occasionally. For an hour every day they step in front of the cameras. Mere snatches of acting. Before every take the French actor invariable repeats to the director: "Don't worry, Jean-Jacques, I understand."

To which the director invariably replies, "Tchéky, make it simpler," for the actor has a tendency to overdo things.

This happens one afternoon when the sun is pounding the rocks. Out of pity, Jack Wallace, as Bill, is finishing off the Airedale wounded by Kaar. The dog plays her part so well that André doesn't have to resort to artifice. Lying on the rock with her face turned toward Philippe's camera, the Airedale is perfectly still while the make-up artist glues strawberry-jam entrails between her legs. "Don't move, don't move," her trainer whispers tenderly.

The camera turns: one shot, two shots, eight shots. Staring into each other's eyes, the Airedale and André seem isolated from everyone else in the crew.

Jean-Jacques knows that the expression he is looking for will come inadvertently. An hour later, the dog lifts her head imperceptibly and offers the desired expression, as if it were a final entreaty.

During that hour, Tchéky tries to concentrate on believing that this dog will actually die. He stares into the sun, forcing tears to well up in his eyes. When Jean-Jacques wants a close-up of his expression, the actor's face is scarlet and puffy from too much exposure to the sun.

"Tchéky, why don't you try to express a more inward sadness?" suggests Jean-Jacques. "If you wish, we'll put tears in your eyes."

"No, no. I wasn't sufficiently moved, and then I overdid it," admits the actor. "But now I definitely feel the scene."

The tears began to appear: one, two, ten. Two seconds of emotion are onscreen, and two more seconds are achieved on August 3, the seventieth day of filming.

A few days later, the crew leaves northern Italy. The minibuses are stuffed, and the trailers for the bears, horses, mules, dogs, cameras, electrical equipment, and canteens dot the Austrian border, heading for the East Tyrol, the small town of Lienz, where the music of a local brass band brings back strange memories. This is postcard Austria: small wooden houses, flowered balconies, winding roads, women and girls wearing lace aprons over their dresses, men wearing leather breeches and Tyrolian hats.

When the crew enters the underbrush on the dawn of August 13, they have only one thing on their minds: their upcoming holiday, which will start at 4:00 P.M. and last two days. A magnificent, incredible, and long-awaited holiday.

Jean-Jacques Annaud is the only one who finds it silly. "A holiday? What for?" he grumbles.

"For nothing," replies the crew in chorus.

"For nothing? What do you mean, 'nothing?' " the director asks.

The camp scene will be finished this evening. Jean-Jacques knows that he has spent three days on shots of the scenery. Pierre is poring over his expense ledger. The amount stuns him: $21.5 million. Being a fatalist, he mutters to himself: "Sometimes you hesitate to buy a dress, and then . . ."

Philippe Rousselot has exerted himself too much during the past few days. He walks around aimlessly, looking drawn and haggard, his hand holding his stomach.

In short, the day starts pretty badly. The director, himself in a bad mood,

sets up for the scene in which *Tom rides away from the camp site followed by Bill.* On the first take, the saddle on which Tchéky sits tips, and the actor falls on the ground. On the second, the horse bolts, leaving his rider behind. On the third, the actor falls before the director can even say, "Action." The crew is bent over laughing. On the fourth take, the miracle finally takes place: rider and horse leave together.

"Jack, could you do the same, please?" asks the director.

Despite intensive training, Jack Wallace has a lot of trouble feeling sure of himself on top of a horse. On the tenth take, Jean-Jacques suggests that he leave on foot, leading the horse by the reins. The director is feeling that this will be a horrible day. During the lunch break the Italian technicians say their final good-byes. A toast is made in their honor. Everyone alleges they will miss one another, and they kiss for the group picture. Then the technicians leave with ceremonial tears in their eyes and real joy in their hearts.

An hour before the wrap, Jean-Jacques says, "Philippe, we're going to film the scene in which Tom undresses."

"That scene! Are you crazy? It will take too long to start setting up for it," answers the sick director of photography.

"We still have so many scenes to shoot," insists Jean-Jacques.

"No, Jean-Jacques. It's no. It would take three hours, and people are going to miss their planes. We won't have enough time."

Besides, the technicians have already started tidying up their materials and putting away the cameras. Seated on a stump, the director is pensive. What is he reflecting on? Is he going to come up with a simpler scene? No, Jean-Jacques Annaud is sulking.

"Good-bye, see you Monday," hum the others.

"Bye," he answers.

Yet Jean-Jacques feels the scene isn't really so complicated. *Tom squats behind a bunch of ferns shimmering with dew. A slight sound makes him lift his head. Graciously emerging in front of him in the morning fog is a doe. She stands completely still and stares at him with her large, gentle eyes and curved lashes.*

Annaud in a quiet moment with Douce.

142

Gradually the set begins to empty. Jean-Jacques remains on his stump. Secretly, he hopes that everyone will come back. Soon the set is deserted. He stands up and heads back to Paris.

Thursday, September 3, 7:00 A.M. Douce is already on the set. It should be said that the cub has not slept much because she spent a good part of the night thinking about her big moment. for weeks she has been dreaming of the great scene in which *Youk confronts the puma:* "How much more time will my director take before coming to the end of this sequence? Of course, the technicians will be excited, but, being tired, one of them is bound to do something stupid. As a result, my associate producer will be anxious, but that's normal, it's his personality. For three weeks now he's been repeating to everyone, 'After this sequence, things will go better.' My director will feel perplexed, though that's not like him. The American trainer will come with Kaar and Bonnie, and we'll have to wait hours for hot wires to be set up, food to be unpacked, and all that cuddling. The feline's trainer, Thierry Leportier, will be so nervous that he'll speak to his puma in a mixture of strange languages, saying hard, stern, severe things that he knows won't be understood. Gogol, one of my stand-ins, will be terribly nervous trying to act as well as I do, Bonnie will be exasperatingly obedient, and I, Douce, will do as I always do: just as I please.

"It's really a pity that the puma has become my enemy. I felt sorry for him because of all the exercises his trainer inflicted on him. Before I got angry with him, when his claws scratched my muzzle, he told me everything about himself. After leaving his comfortable zoo to be taken to his trainer's farm at Rosny-sous-Bois, he told me, he was under such stress from the trip that he didn't stir in his cage for a whole week. But I know it wasn't the trip that disturbed him; it was moving to a new place. Unlike bears, pumas are easily scared. And just to make him more nervous, his trainer named him 'Check-Up.' I've been informed that it means 'complete medical evaluation.' A nice chap, that trainer. He gave him plenty to eat and left him alone. After ten days he opened the cage and wham, he fastened onto him a collar with a lunging rein. My nursemaid would never have dared do such a thing. It's really quite simple: I would have turned down the role. Clearly, since Check-Up didn't bat an eyelid, the trainer took advantage of him. And suddenly in came the stools, from which he had to learn how to jump, every day. When he began to make higher and higher leaps, the trainer stopped. Check-Up thought the training

143

The confrontation scene between the puma and Youk requires the installation of a trunk spanning the river, with a net underneath.

Annaud studies a mock-up of the puma; Xavier Castano stands on the platform.

had reached its end. But wham, next came the trunk, on which he had to climb for weeks. And then the great trip to Austria. Luckily, he brought his girlfriend along, to serve as his stand-in and as his . . . But, I'm getting mixed up. Where was I? Ah, yes, Austria. The set is really large. Check-Up got scared again, what with the river bubbling up everywhere, especially since he hates water. Thank goodness there are a lot of rocks. That's what all that stool-jumping was intended for. And the tree trunk was so much higher than the one he climbed at Rosny-sous-Bois. And tourists went up and down the road trying to get a glimpse of him. Obviously, my director picked a set that he liked. He didn't think of us.

"It's 8:00 A.M. Ah, here they are. With three cameras and their arms full of long metal tubes, tool boxes, safety nets—nice, I'll use them as trampolines— a dinghy, a fake puma paw, jugs of red syrup, a section of a tree, an explosive device, rails . . . I don't know the names for the rest. They dump everything, just like that, on the set, and go have a drink. I look for my director. There he is. He's a bit fuzzy, but that's not his fault; it's my poor eyesight. Another new sweater: when does he find the time to worry about these things? He seems tense, which isn't like him. He should be careful not to bungle this sequence, for it promises to be really spectacular. As far as I'm concerned, I'll do my best to make a success of it, but I'm not alone, there are my co- stars, too. Well, haven't they placed the cameras yet? And haven't they finished staring at the sky? And discussing things with the trainers? It's amazing how much time they spend talking about us. Let's hope Check-Up is in shape to run. But of course he is. With his pinkish-beige robe, he looks like a king. He races down the icy valley. It's incredible how fast he runs. I'm so impressed that I forget it's me he's running after. Fortunately, my director has thought of everything, even having us take turns running in front of the cameras. Otherwise, I wouldn't have been able to see this film to the end.

"Well, now I'm supposed to climb onto this damn tree trunk hanging over the river. It's too high for me; I'm only six months old. It's also a bit scary. It's a strange trunk. It's not as straight as a regular tree. It looks like a dead tree, which might have been replanted horizontally about thirty feet above the water. And the water makes a dreadful noise. The tree is three feet short of the huge rock on the opposite shore. I take a look at the rock and I'm less scared. I see my nursemaid ready to leap, just in case something happens to me. And then, above the water, just under me, there's a net, just in case. My pursuer has arrived. I've climbed faster than he did, but it seems he's not about to leave me alone. He's got a leash under his rump, which his trainer holds in case he feels like getting too close to me. But Check-Up is a coward, as are all the members of his species. He hardly dares stare at me. 'Try a bit harder,' I feel like telling him. In the script, it's a real face-to-face confrontation. My director doesn't know what else to do with him. He's so displeased that he has Check-Up come down the tree, and then he has me step on it. It doesn't make sense. In the script it's the other way around: *The puma advances and Youk draws back*. I've got it: he's afraid I might back away too much and fall down. So he's decided to have the images edited in reverse. Clearly, he could have had me do anything at all. Since he is pleased with me, he has me come down the tree. But what is he doing? He is having the puma go back up again. What about me, then? Am I not performing any longer? Oh, I see. He's filming Check-Up by himself. I think that since he can't do without me in this scene, he's going to link our images together during editing. This way, the spectator will think it's a real confrontation. He's clever, my director.

"Afterward, the make-up artist glues some red liquid on my muzzle and my nursemaid places me on a rock in the river. My director stuffs his arm inside a fake puma paw. What's gotten into him all of a sudden? He brings it closer to my muzzle while growling and making faces. Is he looking for a fight, or what? I don't like this a bit. I wanted to help him do the scene right. He's really upsetting me. I open my mouth. If he continues, I'll jump on him. He's got a lot of nerve. He looks delighted. How stupid can I be? This is exactly what he was looking for. And now he places me on the tree. Strange: the trunk is a bit longer than it was the other day. I am about two feet away from its top. Check-Up follows me, with his leash. I hear a bang. What's this noise? The head set designer seems to be very annoyed. The technicians begin to fret. The explosive charge that is meant to break my tree trunk isn't working. That's movies for you. You do things that are incredibly complicated and then a silly technical detail ruins everything. More wasted hours. I'm discharged. Bang. Bang for the tenth time. Crack.

"Now, I wasn't expecting this, but it worked that time. I fall into the net in the water. It's rather fun at first, but by the third take I've done enough. I pass the baton to my stand-in, Gogol. The scene in the river is all his. But they have to prepare everything. In the water, the technicians install a camera platform at least two hundred feet long, so that the scene can be filmed from Gogol's height. Meanwhile, other technicians assemble air cushions so that the trunk, which has supposedly fallen into the water with me on top of it, does not capsize under Gogol's weight. There's no risk for him. He's the Lilliputian of the bunch and he's certain to drift in the water better than anyone else. They're placing the trunk on the air cushions, and on the trunk they've placed Gogol. But will he float down the river on the branch, all by himself? Of course not. The assistants tie two tick ropes to the cushions so they can guide him wherever my director wishes. In fact, he drifts straight toward the rock where the puma is waiting for him, hungrily. But whatever possessed them to create such a scene? Especially since Check-Up hates water. Gogol, on the

Using a fake puma paw, Annaud simulates an attack on the cub.

The trainer Thierry Leportier instructs the puma to growl.

other hand, loves it. Besides, he keeps jumping off the tree trunk for the sheer pleasure of having a swim. It's nice of my director not to get angry, even though, because they've needed many takes, the sun has moved, and it is necessary to reposition the cameras.

"It's exactly on this day that Claude Berri takes it upon himself to pay us a visit. My poor producer, he must be worried stiff! Right at the moment when Gogol begins to float, I mean without jumping, Check-Up abandons the rock and disappears into the water. So he likes water now? This is certainly not the time for this; the sun is about to set. Crazed, the puma's trainer dives, and discovers the scared puma hiding in a big hole under a rock. It's amazing how much time he makes us waste. My director gets angry; he's right. Ah, finally Check-Up reappears and gets back on his rock. Gogol floats down the river and comes within three feet of him. He's afraid of nothing. For a while

147

it seems that it's Check-Up who's terrorized. Gogol needn't bother getting so close, because, if the idea is to have his face scratched by the puma, I've already played that scene, with my film director as my partner.

" 'Cut!' One of the technicians takes hold of the camera—the only one that filmed everything as planned—and crosses the river. 'Careful,' I shout. 'It moves quickly.' But he doesn't listen. I had predicted that someone would make a stupid mistake. The technician falls into the water. On the bank, my director shouts, 'The film!' Two assistants dive. One of them recovers the camera. Whew! How stupid can he be? He gets a foothold on who knows what and then sinks again. He surfaces once more, disappears again. Help is on the way. The camera is finally fished out. The film is saved. The assistant has lost a tooth; he's a hero.

"Toward the end of the sequence—that is, at the end of ten days—Bart and Bonnie arrive on the set. I don't like Bonnie, with her teacher's-pet airs. Her trainer gives her an order and, pronto, she executes it. That's why they picked her to play Bart's best friend. I ought to be honest about me and Bart: it would never have worked out between us. I'm like my director: I don't take orders from anybody. I am a star. Bonnie is just a very good actress. This didn't prevent her from robbing me of my stardom from time to time.

"Finally, just when Gogol encounters the greatest danger on his floating tree

Claude Berri, the producer, stops by on location.

148

The trainer Christiane d'Hotel is concerned about Douce's safety during the river scene, but in reality it's the puma who is afraid of the cub.

Gogol drifting on a tree limb in the river, facing the camera.

trunk and the puma is about to jump on him, Bart transforms himself into Zorro. He arrives, and the puma is seized with such panic that he leaves the scene. I should also say that he doesn't have much of a choice before such an enormous figure. Besides, he has better things to do. He goes to find his girlfriend. She has never had to work as his stand-in, but she has nothing to regret about the trip: they say she is expecting.

"All of this ended with a nice licking. Kaar was so happy to see Youk again that Bart had to lick Bonnie's face for hours. I was so enervated that I went home to sleep."

The two hunters' long search for Kaar is about to end. The confrontation with the bear is imminent. The whole story as conceived by Brach and Jean-Jacques leads up to this dramatic climax, when man and beast confront each

Bart and Bonnie

other, eye to eye, and measure each other in an irreversible challenge. The authors have spent endless hours writing and rewriting each second of this scene. Tom is going to live through an experience that will transform his entire existence, and for this to be convincing, the tension on the screen must be maximized. The director has conceived very precisely, with the help of drawings, how the scene is to unfold. In building the set, the designers have scrupulously adhered to his specifications. Doug Seus insists on exploring every inch of the area in which Bart is to play his role. But more than anyone else, it is Tchéky who is conscious of the overwhelming responsibility he is shouldering. It's his scene. It is for this very scene that he has, perhaps consciously, perhaps not, agreed to play the role. The weeks he spent climbing the mountains in order to become Tom down to his fingertips do not matter any longer. Nothing matters except these lines in the script: *Tom goes to get some water at a spring. He quenches his thirst with long gulps. He is about to soak his hat in the water. But he freezes on the spot. He turns around and gradually his face becomes distorted in horror. Blocking his path less than thirty feet away, with his jaw wide open, his head swaying with agonizing slowness, Kaar studies his trapped enemy. The way back is cut off. The man is finished.*

On Tuesday, September 15, filming has reached its hundredth day. At Dolomitenhütte, one of the most beautiful tourist spots in Austria, the crew, exhausted by four months of unrelenting work, gets ready to film the most

150

dangerous sequence of a film that has already been through all conceivable tests. Tchéky is on the set at 7:00 A.M. He has not slept for most of the night. Under normal circumstances his concentration tends to be skittish. He is the sort of actor who cannot throw himself into a role unless he lives with it and has been seized by it. He cultivates a certain intensity; that is his style. When he gets too intense, the director must temper his enthusiasm. He gives of himself totally, from the heart.

Three days ago, during an insignificant scene, the two men had this conversation:

"No, Tchéky; you're overacting. I don't understand why you get so frantic."

"But I swear, Jean-Jacques, I really feel that scene deeply."

"Yes, but I don't see the scene in that way."

Tchéky digs his heels in. What Jean-Jacques calls his intensity is his way of identifying with the character he plays. And this time, he thinks, the director is exaggerating. Convinced of his own views, he adds, "But Jean-Jacques, this character has Mexican blood."

"Mexican or not, make it simpler."

Now Tchéky tries hard to appear calm. While the technicians are installing the equipment he inspects his cul-de-sac where the scene takes place, but his eyes are elsewhere. The action will take place in a very confined space, a frighteningly closed-in area for such a memorable confrontation. The set designers have done their job well. The path on which everything takes place is ten feet wide, but its width has been reduced by half to leave the passageway free for hikers, who are still numerous at this time of year: on one side the tourists, and on the other the set. At the edge of the set are fake rocks made of polystyrene, between which runs a cinematic spring. In front is a twenty-square-foot rocky ledge that ends abruptly at a seven-hundred-foot precipice. The way the set is designed, only the precipice is authentic. The technicians try their best to keep the atmosphere relaxed, but Tchéky does not hear their jokes. The danger? In this confined area, it is impossible to install hot wires between him and Bart. But he will not be working without a net. A thirty-by-hundred-foot net has been installed over the edge of the cliff, out of the frame. If the bear becomes unpredictable, the actor will always be able to jump. This may not be enough to put Tchéky's mind at ease, but it allows Jean-Jacques to think that all necessary precautions have been taken.

At 9:00 A.M. everything is set to go, and calmly the director explains the scene to the actor: "You see, you're under the waterfall. You're really enjoying

The confrontation between the hunted and the hunter—with no hot wires separating them, Bart is five feet away from Tchéky Karyo.

quenching your thirst. You're savoring the moment with slow, deliberate gestures. Suddenly you feel a presence behind you. You turn around and see Kaar. You panic and stand flat again the rocky wall. You look for a way out, but in front of you there's only the cliff. You're trapped. You pick up a stone to throw it at the bear, but you realize how ridiculous your gesture is. You're terribly afraid. You hide your head in your arms and curl up. And in a very faint voice, practically a murmur, you say, 'Don't kill me.' O.K.?"

Tchéky takes a deep breath and says, "O.K. I'm ready."

Xavier Castano makes the usual announcemnt: "Attention. No one move. Doug, bring in Bart."

Is it the smallness of the set? This morning the animal seems still larger, stronger, and even more menacing than usual. The trainer takes him precisely to where he is to stand up, then withdraws and hides behind the spring. He orders, "Stand up, Bart."

Bart displays his immense frame. He stands fifteen feet away from the actor, who is absolutely still, with his back to the bear, splashing his face with spring water.

Kaar's shadow on the rocks . . . Tom turns around . . . frightened look . . . the stone in his hand . . . a hasty look toward the precipice . . . Tom falls on his knees . . . curls up . . . begs for mercy . . . "Cut!" Doug comes out from his hiding place inside the fake rock. But Bart does not budge: he is imperial.

Everyone sighs with relief and waits for the director's reaction. Without changing the tone of his voice, Jean-Jacques says, "It's good, Tchéky, but I caught you being frightened of the bear. Now I would like you to play the

152

scene again. I want to see Tom the hunter panic in front of Kaar, not the actor looking toward the camera to see whether the torture session is about to end."

The actor looks at him, flabbergasted, as though he were the victim of a misunderstanding. He knows how difficult the situation is. While mistrusting the animal in reality, he must convey the powerful emotions required by his role. He has trained himself for this. No, Tchéky is not frightened. After witnessing the relationship between Doug and Bart, he knows that the trainer will be able to bring his animal under control at the slightest departure from the script.

Jean-Jacques Annaud smiles without saying anything and gives the go-ahead. Second take, third take: Doug Seus asks for a break. The more relaxed Bart is, the less risky the situation. Gradually the heat becomes more oppressive on this late-summer day. And gradually the confrontation scene finds its ideal intensity. At the sixth take, no one bothers asking whether it is Tom or Tchéky who panics before the bear, but the bear comes so close to the actor that the tension reaches its climax. Suddenly he thrusts his right paw forward, grazing Tchéky's cheek with his claws. He comes so close that Doug is on the verge of jumping in to intervene. Xavier is about to utter a cry.

"Cut. Magnificent," says the director, beaming.

Tom has traveled the heights of humiliation. But that was the desired effect. Tchéky, soaking wet after hours under the waterfall, feels liberated. Further off, Doug offers Bart a pailful of apples. Jean-Jacques takes Tchéky by the shoulders and rubs him with a towel.

"You know," says the actor, convinced of what he is about to say, "if Bart had crossed the line, I think that with one look I would have been able to tame him." One could call this identifying with one's role.

Monday, September 21: by the last five days of filming, the number of technicians has dwindled by half. The English team has already said good-bye. When all was said and done, animatronics represented less than one percent of the film.

This morning Jean-Jacques is to film that last scene of the story: *Kaar and Youk head toward their lair, where they will sleep snuggled next to each other during the long winter months.* On the set, a snowmaking machine spits out thousands of white crystals, which a wind machine swirls. The snow falls on the ground, forming an enormous, fluffy rug.

Suddenly, from nowhere, two people appear. The resemblance leaves no possible doubt: Doug Seus's parents have come to visit their son. At that moment Doug assumes a very busy air, puffing up his chest, asking the director questions regarding the weather forecast for the next two days, taking an inordinate interest in the scenes about to be shot.

The Seuses are very impressed. Papa Seus clasps his big boy impetuously. And Mama Seus rushes toward all the members of the crew, saying in a raspy voice, "Hi, I'm Jean, Doug's mom. How are you?" Then they say hello to the creature who has brought the family joy for so many years. However, this morning Bart is in a foul mood.

Around 1:00 P.M. the technicians leave for lunch, all except Pierre, Doug,

Lynne, Clint, the set photographer, and Jean-Jacques, who has agreed to pose for pictures with Bart. Near the set, with the bear standing behind him, the director sits on a small mound.

From around his neck Jean-Jacques takes his viewfinder, brings it to his eye, pivots, and leans into the animal (a movement that for months he had been warned by Doug might affront the bear). As the photographer starts shooting, the director begins to feel strange vibrations. Simultaneously Doug quickly moves toward the bear. It's too late. The bear throws its two-thousand-pound mass on top of Jean-Jacques. The director has curled himself up as much as possible. His thoughts are racing. Doug has yelled at him not to move and commands the bear, "DON'T TOUCH!"—a command Bart knows all too well. Something has grabbed Jean-Jacques's buttock, but the pain is bearable. Worse is the smell. He has the feeling that an enormous mass of liquid manure had been poured on him. But at the most improbable moment of his life, the director remains lucid.

Five days before filming fin-ishes, Annaud poses with Bart.

Another man might have thought of material things, even ridiculous things, and would let luck decide his fate. Jean-Jacques does what he has always liked to do: he takes a trip. A second later he is in Milan in 1983, with Umberto Eco. Together they relish a statement that the author of *The Name of the Rose* has one of his characters say: "Read, Adso, for the collected knowledge of books has saved many a life." A second later he is on the airplane that is to take him from Los Angeles to Sydney, one day in February 1987. He is immersed in a chapter of *Bear Attacks*. His nose touching the ground, he can just see the page. Third paragraph, fourth line: "In one hundred and five cases of reported grizzly attacks in American parks, the only eight survivors are those who stayed perfectly still and pretended to be dead." Jean-Jacques does not have to read the sentence a second time. He has made up his mind. He will be the ninth survivor. Intensely, passionately, he plays a dead man. For once he has the opportunity to be in a scene; the adventure is exceptional.

Doug Seus, the remarkable professional that he is, stays firm and takes full control. Five seconds later, it's all over. The two-thousand-pound pressure eases, as if Bart's posterior were lifting itself. From between the thick fur the director sees a small gap. The trainer moves down to help Jean-Jacques. Pierre, who thinks a horrible pulp will be lying on the ground, stupefied, watches as legs, a chest, arms, a head extricate themselves from under the hairy mass. It is unbelievable: the body is in one piece, and it works.

Jean-Jacques gets up and slowly moves away toward the canteen. The technicians are just finishing their coffee. The second the film director enters the tent, everyone lifts his head in surprise. His shirt! How did he manage to get it so wrinkled? He is usually so dapper!

"Xavier, can you come with me a minute?" says Jean-Jacques, turning around. The members of the crew let their spoons fall. The back of his trousers are red with blood. Everyone stifles a cry. Jean-Jacques takes Xavier into the other tent.

"Bart jumped on top of me. I think I have a hole in my buttocks; would you mind looking?"

Examining the bleeding, the first assistant feels like throwing up.

"You said a hole; this is enormous, as wide as a ten-franc coin. Not only that, but it seems pretty deep," Xavier says while pouring arnica into the wound. "Aren't your legs shaky? Wouldn't you like to lie down?"

"No, no, I'm perfectly all right," replies Jean-Jacques calmly. Twenty minutes later, the director, who always has a spare set of clothes with him, reappears in the canteen, dapper as ever. While nibbling his food—for all this emotion does leave him feeling hungry—he tells everyone about his accident.

And at 3:00 P.M. filming resumes. Jean-Jacques sets up the scene and hands over the responsibility of filming to Xavier, which gives him time to go to the Lienz hospital. A head of state could not have been given a finer welcome. The necessary services are rounded up by telephone. The entire staff rushes to attend to the wounded buttock of the famous film director mauled by a Kodiak bear, a unique event that day in East Tyrol. Flat on his tummy on the operating table, not knowing a word of German, Jean-Jacques realizes the seriousness of his wound by the effect it has on the men dressed in white. The surgeon takes a piece of gauze and tries to stop the bleeding. Jean-Jacques measures the depth of the wound by observing the unbelievable amount of gauze needed to fill it. He looks at his driver, Hans, and bursts out laughing. With his chest straight as an ancient pillar, Hans clings to his chair and does his best to conform to his reputation: calm and discreet. His body is imperturbable and extremely dignified. But the horrible grimaces he makes with his mouth convey horror and disgust.

Two hours later the director reappears on the set. Stunned, the technicians welcome him with the respect due to the wounded. But Jean-Jacques remains stonily indifferent. Xavier has already begun filming the scene. Filming continues. In short, a day like any other.

The next morning Jean-Jacques arrives on the set at eight o'clock as usual. He limps a bit, but he is as fresh as a bird. Everyone is convinced that he is suffering terribly and would like him once, only once, to break down. The director refuses to give them this pleasure.

Bart is in his cage. Doug starts to plant electric stakes: "Nobody come near. Be careful. Nobody move." Doug's morale is shattered. How can Jean-Jacques explain to this bear trainer from the suburbs of Salt Lake City that he laughed when he remembered that knowledge is the secret of survival? How can he admit that deep down he feels particularly gratified and proud to have shown so much self-control during the crisis? Finally, how can he explain that he considers this incident an amusing experience and that he would not have wanted to trade places with anyone?

For Doug, the consequences of the accident are much more serious. His bear has been a member of his family for nine years, and this is the first time he has attacked anyone. Having previously been dominated, Bart now knows that he can dominate. Doug sees the full extent of the catastrophe. Bart is his livelihood.

The trainer plants the last stake and takes Bart out of his cage. Jean-Jacques picks up the sequence where he left it yesterday: *Kaar and Youk head toward the lair*. Bart must precede the cub. In each take the cub appears in the frame either a second too soon or too late. On the sixth attempt Jean-Jacques gets angry. Doug does not take it well. The atmosphere between the two is tense. The seventh take might have been splendid had the trainer not bobbed into the frame during the shot. At that point Jean-Jacques explodes. Infuriated, Doug takes his bear, puts him into the cage, and begins to put his things away. The director is at his heels. The trainer and the director are nose to nose, shouting. Forever the diplomat, Xavier announces the lunch break.

Doug, his wife, and his son-in-law shut themselves up in their car. All the know-how of Pierre, the cunning of Xavier, and the persuasive skills of Clint are required to coax Doug back. They resume filming. By 3:00 P.M. fog begins to invade the scene. Doug requests that Philippe Rousselot light up the whole mountain so that the bear can see the electric wires. It is difficult to do, but floodlights are set up for each stake. Doug and Jean-Jacques do not speak to each other. Each one does his job. At 5:00 P.M. Bart and the cub end their performances. The Seus family leaves the film set despondently.

The weather next day is very good. Douce gets ready to play her last scene. Ironically, the bear cub is to do the scene in which *Youk, having had a taste of the wonders of civilization, does not want to leave the hunters*. The actors, Tchéky and Jack, are on their horses at a distance. In the foreground Douce sits down, her back to the camera. Action! As though sensing she will never see these men again, the cub stands up to get a better view of them. Her shoulders sag, as if burdened by the weight of enormous sadness. And when the cameras film her from the front, Douce sits down again, rubs her eyes, raises a paw, and says good-bye. The crew does not dare move. Jean-Jacques gets closer to her. Discreetly he places a kiss on the muzzle that has given him so much charm, grace, originality, and tenderness. Then, with thunder booming in the background, the star leaves the set.

It is the last day, September 24. For the director, this day is nothing but the end of one stage of the work. In another week he begins editing the film, something he is particularly eager to do. His desire to see his film is very strong, stronger than it was with his other films at the same stage of production. But first he must finish the filming he started more than four months ago. The

list of scenes that remain to be shot looms very large. Some have to be filmed by day, others by night. The director has foreseen that filming will last from 4:00 P.M. to 2:00 A.M. To liven things up a bit, there are two sets. The first is located on the shore of a lake. Here, the screenplay says, *Joseph, arriving with his dogs on a canoe, draws alongside the camp, where Tom awaits them.* Joseph is played by the French actor André Lacombe. Wearing a pair of rubber-lined trousers that have been boiled to remove most of the dye, a huge, hooded parka, and thick, laced boots, and carrying a foghorn, Joseph has a rumpled, worn look, purposely comical, as if he had not been to a city for many years. The sixty-year-old actor is terribly chatty and totally terrorized by the director.

Designed according to turn-of-the-century specifications, the canoe is superb, but it looks as unstable as it is authentic. In take after take, the Dobermans, the Airedale, and the actor fall into the lake. The pack's trainer can hardly contain his exasperation. Xavier is tired of having to fish out André, who does not know how to swim. The technicians are trying to find a solution.

At 7 P.M. the canoe is nailed to an underwater platform. Beneath this hastily improvised raft, weights keep the platform straight on the surface of the lake. Despite the apparent safety of this system, André gives up. He is replaced by a canoeing instructor. The pack gets on board. Terrified by the barking dogs, the specialist repeatedly forgets to paddle. By the tenth take

Jean-Jacques figures thing have gone far enough. It is then that Xavier comes on the scene. Wearing André's parka, he climbs into the canoe. He is familiar with the dogs, and, as for the screenplay, he can recite it scene by scene. But on the eleventh take the platform capsizes. On the twelfth the dogs dive. The thirteenth is good.

It is 9:00 P.M. The crew goes to have dinner.

Next to the canteen an owl is waiting.

André Lacombe bids everyone farewell. Jean-Jacques actually thanks him. This is a first.

Now filming resumes. The rain falls unobtrusively. On the shore of the lake the campfire irritates Tchéky's eyes. Around the fire the set designers have placed Tom's belongings. The scene is simple: *Tom stands up and limps for ten feet.*

In the first take the actor limps on the wrong leg. "Let's do it over," says Jean-Jacques. One take, two, nine: the actor keeps limping on the wrong leg. Pierre, in a tone inimitably his, interjects, "The animals gave us a hard time, but nothing compared to the actors."

"Tchéky, you're not doing what I'm asking you to do," insists Jean-Jacques.

"But, Jean-Jacques . . ."

"No buts. I'm the director. Lean on the other leg."

"I know you're the director. I think I've already proved it to you," continues the actor, with menacing eyes and trembling lips. Then he stoops, digs his hands into the earth, and adds: "I feel this scene. I feel it. You know I do."

"I don't give a damn what you feel. What matters is what's on the screen."

Tchéky is furious, distraught. He attaches such importance to his feelings that, sometimes, he forgets to play what is in the scene.

Once, before playing a jealousy scene in *Full Moon in Paris*, he said to Eric Rohmer: "To play jealousy, what I'd do is tear up my undershirt and bang my head against the wall." "Oh, no, that's much too complicated for this scene," Rohmer replied. "Well, then I'll just tear my undershirt." "But then you'll have to play the rest of the scene with your undershirt hanging around you," replied the perturbed director.

Tchéky returns to the campfire, his eyes even more irritated by the smoke. He thinks that Jean-Jacques is unfair, but on the tenth take he gets up and limps on the right side for ten feet.

"Let's go; we're moving," says the director.

"Hey, we've still got to do the owl scene," says Philippe. The trainer has been waiting with his bird since 6:00 P.M.

"Let's take them along with us," suggests Jean-Jacques.

It is 1:00 A.M. when they arrive at the other set. With his flashlight Philippe explores the sloping area. The underbrush extends four hundred square feet and borders a swamp.

"It will do," says Philippe. "It's a small area with soft earth and a slippery slope."

He turns to Jean-Jacques, who is looking around excitedly.

"What if, from up there, we lowered a hundred-foot camera platform?"

"Are you crazy? In an hour, filming will be over. Do you know how long it will take to build a hundred-foot platform? Four hours!" answers Philippe, shrugging his shoulders. Then he moves away and begins lighting the area. Tchéky and Jack are sitting around the campfire. The set designers have spread out their belongings. Arnaud and Michele plant their cameras on the edge of the swamp. The technicians are nailing the first planks of the camera platform.

Then the crew has dinner.

Next to the canteen, the owl is waiting.

At 3:00 A.M. Jean-Jacques starts filming. Tom is cleaning his Winchester. Bill is cutting away strips of meat still attached to hides. Two hours later Tom is still cleaning his Winchester, and Bill is trying his very best to find additional pieces of meat to cut off.

At 5:00 A.M. the crew starts another meal.

Next to the canteen, the owl is still waiting.

The crew has finished building the platform. The technicians have performed a marvelous job, a jewel of ingenuity and technical know-how. From atop the platform Michele's camera zooms down on the actors.

At 6:45 A.M dawn is rising between the trees. It is over. Everyone is smiling, except for Jean-Jacques, who seems strangely preoccupied. Surprised, the technicians watch him pace fretfully through the underbrush. What else is he looking for? He heads toward a dense area that daylight has not yet reached and stops in front of a tree, one of whose branches is horizontal. Philippe is on edge. Pierre is puzzled. Arnaud is laughing. Xavier understands. The owl! Suddenly the director asks one of the crew to bring a sheet of black canvas to simulate night and to ask the trainer to come.

Exhausted, the trainer places his owl on the branch. The rehearsal is wonderful.

"Quick! Action! Day is breaking," jokes Jean-Jaccques.

The owl's head pivots 180 degrees.

"Cut. Do it over."

The owl looks straight into the camera. Action! Suddenly the head pivots 125 degrees. The technicians are torn between laughter, total exhaustion, and an unlimited admiration for this relentless determination. This scene is funny and at the same time fascinating. Jean-Jacques has mastered the bears, the cubs, a pack of dogs, and a puma. And yet it is an owl that offers him the most resistance.

On the fifteenth take the owl understands that he had better yield in the face of such obstinacy. He stares, opens his eyes wide, and, to show his cooperation, lets his glottis tremble.

It is 8:22 A.M.

Jean-Jacques Annaud has his seventeen-hundredth scene.

During October 1987, in the Billancourt Studios, film editor Noëlle Boisson finishes cataloging one million feet of film. She has screened the rushes repeatedly and now knows them by heart. She is on the lookout for surprises, enthralled by the diversity of the bear's expressions. Boisson goes beyond a simple narrative flow—she wants to fully comprehend what she is discovering, to analyze the feelings. A system has been set up for sorting, classing, and filing scenes that directly express actions depicted in the script, and additional footage that can be spliced in for a special look, attitude, or gesture has been cataloged as well.

Every day Annaud and Boisson screen ten thousand feet and edit thirty seconds of it. The anxiety increases or decreases depending on the sequence. Because the entire movie has been shot outdoors, there are severe problems in matching the lighting.

Meanwhile, in November, as the picture is being edited, Annaud turns to the soundtrack. In this film it is obvious that sound and music are essential because the storytelling doesn't rely on dialogue at all. It was impossible to record a directly synchronized quality soundtrack during the shooting because the cameras were not always set at the same speed (Annaud used high-speed material for certain expressions) and the trainers had to remain in constant vocal contact with their animals. Therefore the set was an extremely noisy place.

The sound technician had tried to separately record each animal's vocal spectrum. He had spent entire nights making bears and pumas roar, waiting for the cubs' snoring, capturing the owl's hooting, taping the dogs' barking, the crickets' chirping, the faraway waterfalls, the wind . . .

Annaud has hired Laurent Quaglio, one of Europe's most famous sound designers, to be in charge of creating the movie's entire soundtrack. Quaglio's first task is to listen to and sort out the hundreds of sounds recorded during the shooting—a task that will take three months.

In December in Prague, Jean-Jacques meets with Bretislav Pojar, one of the most gifted Czech animated movie creators, whom he had asked a year before to do the dream sequences. Annaud and Pojar choose a spectrum of colors based on Pissarro's and Sisley's paintings for the sweet scenes and on Rouault's and Vuillard's for the more troubled scenes. Almost six months of work by Pojar will ultimately represent forty-five seconds on the screen.

Philippe Sarde begins to work on *The Bear*'s musical score in January 1988. He is proud to work on a movie that has almost no dialogue, a task resembling the one he undertook for *Quest for Fire*. He needs to compose music that prolongs emotions and highlights the story without obscuring it. The musical score must correspond with the imagery of the countryside, which itself was inspired for Annaud by the paintings of the romantic Düsseldorf school. In the end, Sarde creates a theme derived from Eastern European Jewish folklore.

Finally, in March, Jean-Jacques is able to start work in preparation for dubbing the movie. Since it is impossible to have Bart and Douce come to loop their parts, the team builds a sophisticated sound studio in one of the zoo's cages where the full range of bear sounds can be recorded. The first days are quite depressing. One of the males rips up the soundproof carpet and makes a nest out of it; a female pouts and falls asleep in front of the microphone, then refuses to leave the studio for the rest of the week. But after a month, the sound designer finally has a sound library, a catalog of all the desired vocal expressions (growls, rattles, yawns, purrs, roars, and moans), which he integrates into a computer, enabling him to call up the appropriate nuance and duplicate the original sounds recorded during the shooting.

Annaud goes back to the mountains in May for the very last bit of filming. But this time he wants to capture the wonderful, grandiose, and snowy country that he saw in British Columbia for the final images of his movie. He flies over the Yukon in a helicopter, crosses the Arctic Circle, and in the end finds the perfect scenery at the outer reaches of the Beaufort Sea, on the top edge of the Canadian Northwest Territories. The location is about ten hours by helicopter from the last inhabited spot, the Eskimo village of Inuvik.

During the summer the actors dub their ten minutes of dialogue. In the confines of a small 180-square-foot recording studio, they find it difficult to perform their dialogue as if they were in the open air of the mountains. Philippe Sarde has finished scoring the music, and the recording takes place in England with the London Symphony Orchestra.

Boisson and Annaud continue the editing, and the soundtrack dubbing starts. Twenty-two people, divided into four teams, are working on the dubbing. The sounds have been computerized for selecting, adjusting, and synchronizing them with the picture. The job of meshing the sounds of the footsteps goes on with two teams for five weeks—five times longer than usual. Then it is time for pre-mixing, when the bears' dialogue and the sound effects are blended and balanced before the final mixing with the music—a task that takes ten times longer than usual.

It is not until September 20, 1988 that the 70-mm version with six-track Dolby stereo is ready.

On October 19, 1988, four hundred movie theaters throughout France show *The Bear*. Twenty-four days later, the film has been viewed by a million moviegoers in Paris, setting a new record.

From November 1988 to July 1989, the movie comes out in Switzerland, Belgium, Italy, Spain, Norway, Sweden, Greece, Germany, Austria, Finland, Holland, Portugal, Africa, the West Indies, Morocco, Hong Kong, Denmark, Japan, and New Zealand. In twelve European countries the movie grosses more than $100 million.

THE BEAR
Credits

PRICE ENTERTAINMENT
presents
a **CLAUDE BERRI** Production
a **JEAN-JACQUES ANNAUD** Film
Screenplay by
GERARD BRACH
based on "The Grizzly King" by **JAMES OLIVER CURWOOD**

The Cast
BART
the Kodiak bear
YOUK
the bear cub
JACK WALLACE
TCHEKY KARYO
ANDRE LACOMBE

Film Editor	NÖELLE BOISSON
Sound Designer	LAURENT QUAGLIO
Music by	PHILIPPE SARDE
Director of Photography	PHILIPPE ROUSSELOT
Production Designer	TONI LUDI
Production Manager	LEONHARD GMUER
Associate Producer	PIERRE GRUNSTEIN
Produced by	CLAUDE BERRI
Directed by	JEAN-JACQUES ANNAUD

All scenes depicting injury to
animals have been simulated.

DOUG SEUS' WASATCH ROCKY
MOUNTAIN WILDLIFE, INC.

Bear Trainers	DOUG SEUS
(Bart and Youk)	LYNNE SEUS
	CLINT YOUNGREEN
Biological and Storyboard Consultant	DOUG SEUS

STEVE MARTIN'S WORKING
WILDLIFE

Bear Trainers	MARK WEINER
(Doc and Grizz,	Keith Bauer
Stand-In Bears)	Madeleine Klein
Zoological Advisor	JEAN-PHILIPPE VARIN
	Jacana Wildlife Studio
Veterinarians and Scientific Advisors	FRANCOIS HUGHES
	MARYVONNE LECLERC-CASSAN

Wild Grizzly Consultant	DOUG PEACOCK
Bear Cub Trainers	CHRISTIANE D'HOTEL
	CARLO DO COUTO
	Marie-France Gaboret
	Danilo Gobber
	Nathalie Laforge
	Patrick Bleuzen
	Maguy Fernandez
	Claude Charat
	Didier Bongibault
	NOEL VANDENDRIES-LESTIENNE
	Sonia Vandendries-Lestienne

DIETER KRAML and his bears
Alfons Spindler and his bears

Puma Trainers	THIERRY LEPORTIER
	Monique Angeon
	Gilbert Weiser
Dog Trainers	ANDRE NOEL
	Patrick Pittavino
	Jean-Alain Kerfriden
Horse Trainers	ANDREAS NEMITZ
	Sue Bushell
	Bernard Heinrich
Stunt Horse Trainers	MARLO LURASCHI
	Christian Henning
Falconer	JOSEPH HIEBELER
1st Assistant Director	XAVIER CASTANO
Assistant Directors	ISABELLE HENRY
	Philippe Raths
	Florian Nilson
Art Directors	HEIDI LUDI
	Antony Greengrow
	Georg Dietz
Costumes	CORINNE JORRY
	Françoise Disle
Make-up	HANS-JURGEN SCHMELZLE
Locations Scout	NORBERT PREUSS
Construction	FRANZ BAUMGARTNER
Prop Master	BERNHARD HENRICH
Prop Man	JIRI JUDA
Weapons	KARL NEFZER

Special Effects	WILLY NEUNER		Irene Gross
	Uli Nefzer	Location Production	
	Johann Fickel	Managers	CARLO MARGRAF
Mountain Guides	LEO BAUMGARTNER		Alfred Deutsh
	MAX MUTSCHLECHNER	Animal Management	JACQUES ALLAIRE
Worldwide Press and			Albrecht Von Bethmann
Marketing	JOSEE BENABENT-		Walter Pucker
	LOISEAU	Financial	
Assisted by	Alex Nouveau	Controller	PIERRE TREMOUILLE
Storyboard	LAURENCE DUVAL	Production	
Drawings	NORBERT IBORRA	Accountants	HELGA PATRY-PLOINER
Cameraman	ARNAUD DU		COLETTE SUDER
	BOISBERRANGER		Hannes Patry
			Trixi Waizenauer
1st Camera		Production	
Operator	MICHELE PICCIAREDDA	Secretaries	JACQUELINE TOLIANKER
Camera Assistants	RINO BERNARDINI		Virginie Petit
	Myriam Touzé		
	Jérôme Peyrebrune		
	Andreas Gerbl		
	Barthélémy Bogaert		
Video	IAN KELLY	**Post Production**	
Opticals	FREDERIC MOREAU	Second Unit Editor	ANNE LAFARGE
	PATRICE BEAUD	First Assistant	
	(Euro-Titres)	Editor	MICHELE HOLLANDER
Animation	BRETISLAV POJAR	Assistant Editors	ANNE MANIGAND
	Studio Kratky Film (Prague)		Danièle Fillios
	Ceskoslovensky Filmexport		Bénédicte Nambotin
Continuity	Claude Luquet		Claire Sels
	Marie-Florence Roncajolo	Sound Editors	ERIC MAUER
	Katharina Enger		FABIENNE ALVAREZ
Casting	Mary Jo Slater (USA)		Roberto Garzelli
	Elisabeth Leustig (USA)	Assistant Sound	
	Susan Willett (USA)	Editor	Corinne Rozenberg
	Valérie Marcou (FRANCE)	Footsteps	
Behavior Coordinator	AILSA BERK	Artists	JEAN-PIERRE LELONG
Body Movements	BALDWYN		Mario Melchiori
	Roman Stefanski	Mixing	CLAUDE VILLAND
	Dave Forman		BERNARD LEROUX
	Michael Blair	Post-Synchronization	GERARD LEDU
Expressions	ROBERT TYGNER		JEAN-FRANÇOIS AUGER
	MAK WILSON		Denis Carquin
	Simon Buckley	Technical Department	Véronique Boucheny
	Philipp Eason	Music Consultant	ERIC LIPMANN
	Don Austen	Additional Music	LAURENT QUAGLIO
	Clint Youngreen		ERIC MAUER
U.S. Consultants	Monty Diamond	Orchestration by	BILL BYERS
	Pierre Andrieux		ALEXANDER COURAGE
	(Gag Productions)	LONDON SYMPHONY ORCHESTRA	
English Script		Conducted by	CARLO SAVINA
Collaboration	JOHN BROWNJOHN	Color Timing	OLIVIER CHIAVASSA
Additional Dialogue	Sandy Whitelaw		YVAN LUCAS
Unit Manager	JANOU SHAMMAS	Animatronic bears created by	
Location		JIM HENSON'S CREATURE SHOP	
Managers	MARLENE VANTHUYNE	Production	
	Sonja Beutura	Supervisor	JOHN STEPHENSON
	Kurt Von Vietinghoff	Creative Supervisor	CHRIS CARR

About the Filmmaker

JEAN-JACQUES ANNAUD is the award-winning director of *Black and White in Color* (1976), *Hothead* (1979), *Quest for Fire* (1981), *The Name of the Rose* (1986), and *The Bear* (1988). *Black and White in Color* won an Academy Award for Best Foreign Language Film in 1977; *Quest for Fire* was awarded two Césars in 1982—for Best Film and for Best Director; and in 1987 *The Name of the Rose* received a César for Best Foreign Film.

Annaud was born in Draveil, outside of Paris, on October 1, 1943. After attending the Sorbonne and the Higher Institute of Cinematographic Studies, he became one of the top television commercial directors in France, making nearly 500 commercials, which have been honored with numerous international prizes.

About the Author

JOSÉE BENABENT-LOISEAU has worked in movie publicity and marketing for seventeen years with such studios as Paramount, Universal, and MGM, and with such directors as Claude Berri, Steven Spielberg, Milos Forman, Roman Polanski, Francis Ford Coppola, John Boorman, Federico Fellini, and Jean-Jacques Annaud. Ms. Benabent-Loiseau was involved with *The Bear* through its entire six-year odyssey. She makes her home in Paris.

Newmarket Press Presents Two Movie Tie-ins To *The Bear*

THE BEAR—A NOVEL

(Originally published as *The Grizzly King*)

by James Oliver Curwood

Introduction by Jean-Jacques Annaud, director of the film *The Bear*

The original novel that inspired the spectacular film is now in print in a movie tie-in edition for readers of all ages. This classic about an orphaned bear cub, a mighty grizzly, and the two men who hunt them in the Rocky Mountains of 1885 British Columbia remains as fresh and stirring as the day it was written. With remarkable insight into animals, Curwood, one of America's most popular adventure writers, ranked with Jack London and Zane Grey, reveals to us that "the greatest thrill of the hunt is not in killing, but in letting live." "Spellbinding—a sure hit in all media. Curwood's long-forgotten novel turns out to be as thrilling as the movie."—*The Kirkus Reviews*. Available in both hardcover and paperback. 208 pages, 10 photos.

THE ODYSSEY OF THE BEAR

The Making of the Film by Jean-Jacques Annaud

by Josée Benabent-Loiseau

Illustrated with 100 photos, this behind-the-scenes look at the movie that has become one of the most successful films ever released answers the most often-asked question, How on earth did they do it? Josée Benabent-Loiseau has reconstructed 6 years of meticulous preparations and 19 weeks of filming in the Italian Dolomites. Showing the sometimes dangerous, sometimes humorous situations of working with wild animals, this well-paced volume proves to be a memorable story in its own right. "*The Bear* is the most ambitious animal flick ever made. The story behind the making of *The Bear* is as fascinating as anything that appears on screen."—Mike McGrady, *Newsday*